Great Houses of
SUMMIT AVENUE
and the Hill District

Great Houses of
SUMMIT AVENUE
and the Hill District

KAREN MELVIN

Photography by
KAREN MELVIN

Foreword by
GARRISON KEILLOR

Introduction by
PAUL CLIFFORD LARSON

Text by
PAUL CLIFFORD LARSON
BETTE JONES HAMMEL
MELINDA NELSON
DAVE KENNEY

Illustrations by
NARDA LEBO

www.summitavenuebook.com

Printed in China

10 9 8 7 6 5 4 3 2

International Standard Book Number
ISBN: 978-0-9892627-0-5

Library of Congress Control Number: 2013946172

Book design by Ellen Huber
Copy-editing by E. B. Green Editorial, St. Paul

COVER IMAGE: *Carlos N. Boynton House.*

PREVIOUS PAGE: *Financier William W.
Bishop's house is a Queen Anne confection
at the heart of Summit Avenue's long stretch
of Victorian-era residences. Built in 1887, its
designer was George Wirth, the first of the
city's elite corps of Eastern-trained architects
to arrive in St. Paul.*

Big
Picture
Press

To my loving husband, Phil
—KM

Contents

FOREWORD

by Garrison Keillor

The folks who built the big houses on Summit Avenue from Civil War days onward were keen to get up away from downtown St. Paul, whose clamor and stink was a byproduct of the prosperity that allowed them to move up and away from it into great stone and brick mansions overlooking a steep slope to the simple frame houses of their workers. They were railroad men, lumbermen, manufacturers, wholesalers, and on Summit Avenue they could get far away from the rails, the sawmills, the factories, and live in the elegance, even opulence, to which they felt richly entitled.

James J. Hill, for example, had come to the city as a mere clerk, worked his way up, taken big chances, and ridden horseback through the Rockies to lay out his Great Northern Railway by the time his new home was complete. He heartily enjoyed his prosperity, his family vacations in Paris, and his great Victorian castle with art gallery, pipe organ, and greenhouse.

The mansions of Summit were intended to declare the owners' status in St. Paul society—you could drive by and see the porte cochere, the colonnade, the turret, and you knew that the owner had not just fallen off the turnip wagon. Eventually the owners faded and died—so many of them, including the Hills, were not a long-lived lot—and their fortunes were divvied up. Their heirs hoofed it out of town, and the old mansions—chopped into rooming houses or abandoned and gently decaying—sat until the great wheel of fashion turned in the 1970s and '80s, when renovating historic homes became a cool thing to do. Scores of young couples set out to do that and so saved the avenue. Otherwise it might have become a boulevard of hair salons, wine bars, and knickknack shops, and the city would have lost something rather elegant.

What remains on Summit today has almost nothing to do with Hills, Weyerhaeusers, Ordways, or Schunemans, or with anyone's social status, real or imagined. What remains and is so clear in Karen Melvin's lovely pictures is the fine workmanship of the buildings,

the stonework and brickwork and wood carving and cabinetry and carpentry of thousands of anonymous men, many of them immigrants, who rode the streetcars or climbed up the hill from the flats, carrying their lunch buckets, to work on the construction crews six days a week, ten hours a day.

James J. Hill, of 240 Summit, was the most famous resident; after him was Sinclair Lewis, a radical among the tycoons, who lived in 516 for a year. Then came the 24-year-old writer who hit it big with his first novel—completed in the attic of 599 Summit—who left town in 1922 and never returned. Never, so far as we know, had he any urge to return. Nonetheless, his readers still hike up and down Summit looking for signs of F. Scott Fitzgerald, the perpetual youth and outsider, gazing at the lighted windows of great houses and daydreaming about the grand lives lived there.

What the residents of Summit see now as they look out their windows is the leafy boulevard of a bygone time, where you could shoot scenes of a movie about jowly tycoons in linen suits and their rambunctious offspring, with a dotty uncle, a rakish suitor, and a bevy of Irish housemaids tossed in. A grand old Victorian street, drowsy on a summer afternoon.

Then four young women in short shorts come jogging by, their ponytails bouncing, and then a tour group led by a lady with a clipboard, who stops them for a brief talk about the characteristics of Gothic Revival. The phone rings and you are back in the present, and it is the plumber, who says he's on his way. No matter how grand the exterior of the house, we all have to deal with the basics of life. In other words, plumbing.

Great Houses of
SUMMIT AVENUE
and the Hill District

INTRODUCTION

by Paul Clifford Larson

ummit Avenue—park, promenade, and prolonged residential neighborhood rolled into one—is a marvel of high Victorian urban planning. Minnesota's early promoters were quick to see the potential of the bluffs and ridges overlooking the city of St. Paul and the Mississippi River, but the splendid boulevard there today was a long time coming. When statehood arrived in 1858, just half a mile of Summit Avenue, running from what is now Kellogg Boulevard to Western Avenue, was laid out. Six houses stood in two small clusters. Four years later, James Burbank moved a quarter mile farther out, stretching the avenue a few hundred yards.

Burbank's mansion, an architectural showpiece set within an extensive, managed landscape, was the first to realize the ideal of the state's visionary propagandists, but it failed to inspire peers. The avenue's development sputtered through the 1860s and 1870s, its roadbed remaining little more than a wagon rut with the Burbank estate its outpost. In late spring 1883, *The Northwest* magazine bemoaned: "St. Paul has no pleasant promenade street with wide sidewalks and ample roadway, but Minneapolis has a dozen of them."

Hardly had that issue gone to press when changes occurred with a rapidity astonishing eastern visitors. In fall 1883, St. Paul newsmen cited Bradstreet's report that the city's expenditure on building improvements trailed only New York, Chicago, and Cincinnati, cities whose populations dwarfed St. Paul's 75,000 residents. Summit Avenue rose with the tide, the neighborhoods on either side became the most fashionable quarter of the city, and the city complied by supplying them with water before the line was run to downtown businesses.

Well-heeled residents of Lowertown joined with new residents of the city, forsaking the clamor of their old quarter for an avenue more elevated in geography, ambience, and social status. Among those who could easily afford life on the hill were those feasting off the booming population of Minnesota and points west. Prominent among them were railroad magnate James J. Hill and lumber baron Frederick Weyerhaeuser. Self-styled "capitalist" William W. Bishop settled on the avenue in 1887, with fellow land speculators Charles L. Johnston and Carlos N. Boynton arriving in the following century. Another class of incoming residents enjoyed profits from businesses that grew up with the city. Among the best known were dry-goods merchants George Finch, Samuel Dittenhofer, A. W. Lindeke, and the Goodkind brothers, along with insurance man Frederick Fogg and energy executive Paul Doty. These were joined by residents of somewhat lesser means, as mini-neighborhoods of upper-echelon white-collar workers such as railroad clerk W. W. Howard intermingled with the rows of palatial homes.

To put substance to the dreams of these men and their families, two generations of architects flooded in from the East Coast as well as from England and Germany.

TOP: *This bird's-eye view of Summit Avenue in 1883 shows the Burbank mansion and carriage house at the lower left, Norman Kittson's mansion at the upper right, and the houses perched on the still-rugged terrain between.* ABOVE: *James C. Burbank's estate at the end of Summit Avenue, as shown in* Andreas's Illustrated Historical Atlas of Minnesota *in 1874. The boardwalk was exclusive to his house.*

Fourteen immigrant architects and a score of eastern practitioners moved to St. Paul during the building boom of the 1880s, and many of them found patrons and places to display their art on Summit Avenue. Leading the way in the 1880s was German-born but American-trained George Wirth, with sometimes St. Paul residents Clarence H. Johnston and Cass Gilbert soon to follow. Each of these, like a score of their peers, had spent time in the office of pioneer architect Abraham Radcliffe, whose generation had clearly passed the torch. Radcliffe's supreme achievement on Summit Avenue, the Norman Kittson mansion of 1882–84, was out of date before it was complete. It also proved short-lived, yielding its site at the head of the hill to the Cathedral of Saint Paul after just 22 years.

Other architects brought diversity and depth to Summit Avenue's growing legacy. Allen H. Stem, J. Walter Stevens, and Emmanuel Masqueray achieved national standing for railroad buildings, warehouses, and churches respectively, but each had some of his finest moments as a designer in the neighborhoods embracing Summit Avenue. Through the first two decades of the 20th century, a third generation of architects—most notably Minneapolis's Prairie School partnership of Purcell and Elmslie—found opportunity to do some their best work on and near Summit Avenue.

Joel Whitney's sled-dog photo of 1859 shows six mansions along Summit Avenue facing south over the present-day Seven Corners area—only the one at 312 Summit still survives.

At the outset of the boom, public attention on the avenue focused entirely on enlargement and enhancement of the boulevard, with little regard for its standing architecture or the burst of new building activity. As early as 1872, eminent landscape architect Horace Cleveland argued that the building of mansions on the south side of the avenue had defaced its public value by obliterating the magnificent bluff view. His vision of shared, panoramic scenic views from the boulevard found its single fruition in a small plot known as Summit Lookout (now Overlook Park), at the bend near where the University Club arose.

City directories from 1903 to 1921 closed their introductions with a paean to the "beautiful Summit Avenue Boulevard, with its shifting panorama of the river and sky, of old ivy-covered walls and green fields far away." But by this time, the scenic value of the avenue was understood to embrace its "magnificent homes in every fancy of architectural renaissance." The shift in focus from creating a greenway to celebrating its architecture was underway. The avenue and its buildings were, in the eyes of the public at large, a treasured public resource.

The first city-sponsored efforts to preserve the architectural character of Summit Avenue occurred in 1915, when St. Paul passed its first zoning ordinances to keep businesses

Norman Kittson's Second Empire fantasy was the most lavish house on Summit Avenue until James J. Hill arrived. It was demolished and replaced by the Cathedral of Saint Paul in 1905.

and other incompatible uses at bay. But as the wealthy moved away from the older part of Summit, the division of their homes into multiple units was inevitable. The World War I era brought a wave of duplexing, and this intensified to four-plexing in the wake of World War II.

By 1960 nearly three quarters of the housing units east of Dale Street were renter-occupied. Romanticists of Summit Avenue's glorious past were hanging on by their fingernails. Newsperson Kathryn Boardman characterized the avenue as "a kind of Marlene Dietrich of a street, with everlasting magic" no matter its sags and wrinkles. She was in fact on the fringes of a new preservation ethic, defining the value of the avenue as a historic rather than a scenic resource.

From the late 1960s until the early 1980s, the nonprofit Old Town Restorations, Inc., was instrumental in buying, selling, and restoring homes and in educating St. Paul residents about preservation. Lasting protection for Summit Avenue's architectural heritage arrived in 1976, when the Hill District became the first preservation district in St. Paul. That same year it achieved national status as the largest historic district in the country on the National Register. Three separate citizens' organizations—the Ramsey Hill and Summit Hill Associations and the Summit Avenue Residential Preservation Association—arose to monitor, protect, and preserve the historic character of the avenue and its neighborhoods.

Preservation activity would have had little point had Summit Avenue not retained much of its integrity through decades of economic and social challenge. The avenue's survival as a prized architectural landscape has outlived its Victorian beginnings largely because it found ways to accommodate to a changing world. Such accolades as "the best-preserved American example of the Victorian monumental residential boulevard" and the "best intact street from the Victorian Era" short-change the breadth of the avenue's achievement. Until recent times, there was nothing sacrosanct about 19th-century houses. Successive waves of fashion replaced or altered past recognition scores of mansions between the building boom of the 1880s and the period revivals of the Roaring Twenties. Most of Summit Avenue beyond Lexington Parkway consists of 20th-century residences.

St. Paul's long refusal to allow Summit Avenue to remain riveted in time is the key to the wealth of its legacy. All of the great Victorian streets of the Midwest—from Euclid Avenue in Cleveland and Prairie Avenue in Chicago to Park Avenue in Minneapolis and Trost Boulevard in Kansas City—radiated from their downtown cores. Only Summit Avenue enjoyed a terrain isolating it from commercial growth. Only Summit continued to renew itself over three generations. And only Summit Avenue has survived with more than a ghost of its former grandeur.

1858 | STUART–DRISCOLL HOUSE

312 SUMMIT AVENUE   *by Dave Kenney*

I f you really want to appreciate the architectural significance of the Stuart-Driscoll house, consider a certain photograph that Joel E. Whitney—St. Paul's first commercially successful photographer—took on a winter's day in 1859. In the foreground (see page 4) is a sled-dog team at rest near what we now call West Seventh Street. In the background, perched on the bluff, are some of the grandest homes of early St. Paul. Only one of those homes—the one on the far left with the cupola— still exists. The Stuart-Driscoll House is the oldest surviving home on Summit Avenue.

Built for lumber dealer David Stuart in 1858 during a nationwide economic depression, "Stuart's Folly" was a stucco-covered, Italian Villa-style mansion that its financially strapped owner probably wished he had never begun. Stuart died shortly after construction was complete, but his house has survived and evolved. In 1887 its new owner, St. Paul mayor Robert A. Smith, hired the firm of architects Cass Gilbert and James Knox Taylor to oversee a major remodel. Apparently the work was complete in time for Smith to host a lunch in the mansion's "commodious dining room" for President Grover Cleveland, who stopped in the Twin Cities during a tour of midwestern states.

About 30 years later, another owner—St. Paul businessman Arthur B. Driscoll—engaged architect Thomas Gannett Holyoke to design a three-story rear addition, which may have included partial renewal of the original roof cupola. In the years that followed, the house—with ample space to accommodate multiple boarders—was rarely vacant. Its ability to generate rental income helped it survive, even as other homes of its era succumbed to hard times.

Steve and Judy Balej knew little of the home's history when it hit the market in early 1989. They were on the lookout for a Summit Avenue house and had come close to purchasing one across the street, but they hadn't considered looking at 312. "I came here reluctantly," Steve says. "I did not like stucco houses. I liked brick, and I liked brownstone and all that kind of stuff. But I said to Judy, 'Okay, let's go look at the ugly stucco house with the gold lanterns.'" Once they stepped inside, their skepticism vanished. "I got to the center of the house, and I knew in less than a minute that this was the one," Steve recalls. "The staircase—I looked at that, and I went, 'Oh my God! Look at that! This is it!'"

OPPOSITE: *With its main doors open to both front and back, the oldest home on Summit Avenue remains a welcoming presence. The identity of the original architect is unknown.*
ABOVE: *In 1887 the house retained its original balustrade-lined front porch and second-floor terrace.*

OPPOSITE AND ABOVE: *The grand staircase was reworked—and possibly shifted from its original location—during an 1880s remodeling by the architectural firm of Cass Gilbert and James Knox Taylor.* LEFT: *Three historically appropriate light fixtures, installed by the previous owner, illuminate the central hallway.*

OPPOSITE: *The wood-clad first-floor library, which suffered major damage when a water pipe burst several years ago, has been fully restored.* FOLLOWING PAGES: *President Grover Cleveland lunched in the home's wood-paneled dining room during a visit in 1887.*

As Steve and Judy quickly realized, the house's plain, gray façade masks a stunning interior. The centerpiece staircase that initially caught Steve's eye sits beneath a magnificent glass chandelier and spills into the main hallway and foyer. The hallway, in turn, leads to a succession of well-preserved rooms. The sunny front parlor, resplendent in formal cream-on-white, almost certainly served as a reception room for the "lady of the house" during the 1800s and early 1900s. The wood-clad library, across the hall, brings to mind politicians and businessmen laughing over cigars and brandy. The living room, with its Ionic columns, 13-foot-high ceilings, and dancing-floor dimensions, conjures scenes of private concerts and guests in formal attire.

The grand piano, fitting comfortably into the oversized bay, recalls the annual jazz parties that in more recent years Steve and Judy threw for family and friends. The dining room's finely crafted wood features—its paneled walls, 30-inch coving, and hand-cut flooring—exude a solidity that President Cleveland might well have enjoyed when he lunched there more than a century ago.

Over the years, Steve and Judy were careful not to compromise the house's historical integrity. The few changes they made were carefully considered. They put off restoring an upstairs bathroom until they could find vintage tile that precisely matched the original ceramic work. They returned bookcases and light fixtures scattered through the house to their original locations, using vintage photographs as guides.

Beyond that, they left the main floor almost exactly as it looked when they first moved in—as if the house, with its long and distinguished history, were teaching them to appreciate its past. "I was a suburban kid who knew nothing about history," Steve says. "I learned from a previous project that it's better to wait than to forge ahead with a remodeling project and do it wrong."

The owners' appreciation for the house's history is impossible to miss. Judy, who died in 2011, was known as a gracious host who welcomed tour groups and even casual passersby into her home. "People would be outside, and she'd ask, 'Would you like to come in?'" Steve says. "And of course, they'd respond, 'We'd love to!'"

As one of few Summit Avenue homes with a reputation for being open to the public, the Balej home is no private museum. Instead it has settled into a comfortable life as a piece of living history enjoyed by its owners and others, too. As Steve puts it, "Judy and I always felt we were caretakers for the time we were here."

OPPOSITE AND BELOW: *Musical motifs over the fireplace suggest that this elongated space with piano-accommodating bay was originally designed as a performance space. Classical ornamentation of Ionic columns, 13-foot ceilings, and ornate moldings were common to pre-Civil War architecture.*

RIGHT: *During its early years, the front parlor probably served as a reception room for the "lady of the house."*

by Paul Clifford Larson

The first grand estate built on Summit traverses the arc of period fashion like no other on the avenue. Its story begins during the Civil War, when James C. Burbank (1822–1876) accumulated enough capital from his express business to move from the bustling commercial center of the city to a place where he could stretch his legs. He chose an expansive property on a meandering, bluff-top carriage path that was still a long way from becoming the pride of the city. Several neighbors occupied two clusters of houses a half mile closer to downtown.

Rather than trust the still thin stock of talent in a fledgling prairie city, Burbank sought the services of Otis L. Wheelock, a front-rank Chicago architect. Wheelock created a dramatically sited Italian villa—or as one historian put it, "at least an American romanticized conception of one." The local press crowed that it was "a splendid architectural ornament" that "would grace the finest streets of New York." The rustic character of local limestone only added to its romantic effect—a mansion carved from St. Paul's bedrock. Organized around a central hall in typical midcentury fashion, it was ventilated by an ornamental belvedere crowning the roof. Among the first houses in St. Paul to boast steam heat, hot and cold water, and gas lighting, it also had an air chamber between stone walls and brick lining to retard the entry of frost and rats. The cost exceeded $20,000, a princely sum for its day.

OPPOSITE: *The Burbank–Livingston–Griggs House commands its site with the same quiet authority it did in 1863. Built of limestone quarried across the river, it sports all the elements of the Italianate style, including a belvedere that doubled as the central component of the house's ventilating system.* ABOVE: *The fireplace of the "stone room" at the rear of the house is intricately carved in Italian Renaissance style.*

At the end of the war, Burbank moved on to reorganize and head the St. Paul Fire and Marine Insurance Company, occupying new quarters downtown as lavish as those at his home. By then one of the wealthiest men in the city, Burbank and his household in 1870 included one Irish and two Swedish domestics, a coachman, a gardener, and a driver, plus his wife, Evelyn Delano Burbank, and their three daughters. The male servants resided in an elegant carriage house at the rear of the property.

The grandeur of the home failed to suffice for its succeeding owners. Four times over the course of 50 years starting in 1883, they brought in the finest of St. Paul's architects to nudge the house to current standards. Her health failing, Burbank's widow sold the house to St. Paul dry-goods merchant George R. Finch (1839–1910), who immediately hired rising 24-year-old architect Clarence Johnston to bring the interior of the house to the level of its Summit Avenue neighbors. In an unsigned newspaper article, Johnston's peer and friend

Cass Gilbert had declared the mansion "simply a large square house" that was "very much out of date," despite its commendable "suggestion of calm dignity and repose."

In his $15,000 remodeling ($400,000 in current dollars) for Finch, Johnston created a breathtaking stair hall, 25 feet in each dimension, with a second-floor gallery circling the hall. He also replaced the two tall windows on the stair landing with an elegant triptych, using glass that was stained, as he put it, "in opal and Venetian antique colors." During his years in New York working for the Herter Brothers, Johnston had fallen under the sway of the Aesthetic movement, and he was quick to introduce to St. Paul its emphasis on the design of artful architectural environments. A decade later he returned at the call of new owner Crawford Livingston (1846–1925) to replace the elaborate porch piers and bracketry with up-to-date Neoclassical columns.

When the house passed to Livingston's daughter, Mary Griggs (1879–1967), in the aftermath of World War I, it underwent a virtual implosion of interior changes. The first order of business was hiring Allen H. Stem to create a new living room overlooking the gardens. His "stone room" is the transformation of an open porch into an elegant lounging space done in English Renaissance fashion, with an Italian fireplace and a strap-and-scroll-work plaster ceiling.

Five years later, at the onset of the Great Depression, Mary Griggs collaborated with architect Edwin Lundie and Venetian architectural antiques dealer Adolph Loewi to implant 18th-century French and Italian interiors in the original living room (now the salon), dining room, three bedrooms, two sitting rooms, wardrobe room, and a small hallway. Lundie may have been the only architect in the state willing and able to slave over fitting the historic rooms into their new locations and matching colors with 300-year-old patinas. First completed was the salon, a room lined with mirrors and painted in soft shades of green and gold. Like the rooms to follow, it realized Griggs and Lundie's vision of "something wonderfully different."

Johnston's triumphant staircase and monumental entry hall and Stem's capture of the Renaissance in the stone room remained unscathed as wonders enough in themselves. Griggs's sole touch in the former was replacement of the stained glass in the window triptych with the coats-of-arms of her and her husband's families, surrounded by clear leaded glass.

Mary Livingston Griggs's daughter, Mary Griggs Burke, gave the house to the Minnesota Historical Society in 1968, hoping it would continue as a "living house" rather than as a museum. Though its use for offices and sporadic social occasions fell short of those wishes, the house was kept alive but awaiting a full restoration. In 1996 the property passed to Commonwealth Properties, a St. Paul developer and manager of historic buildings. Under the management of John Rupp, the house has been lovingly restored and converted to apartments, maintaining the historical integrity of each room and floor.

OPPOSITE, TOP AND BOTTOM:
Mary Griggs hired Edwin Lundie to place
18th-century French and Italian interiors
into several rooms of the house. The
casework of the dining room was carefully
fitted around murals by the Baroque
Flemish painter Jan Frans van Bloemen,
commonly known as Orrizonte. ABOVE
AND RIGHT: *The salon (above) posed*
special difficulties for Lundie. Not only
did the paintings barely fit into the spaces
between the windows, but also the woodwork
had a complex greenish patina that took
the architect hours to match. Even in a
comparatively simple installation like
the bedroom (right), each panel and piece
of trim and molding had to be cut or
augmented to fit into its new location.

ABOVE AND LEFT: *Multiple entry-hall vantage points reveal Johnston's shaping of interior space to be as inventive as his craftsmen's carving of the woodwork.*
OPPOSITE: *Architects and craftsmen of the 1880s freely exploited ornamentation from earlier periods. Johnston mined them all to deliver everything from Neoclassical diaper patterns, dentils, and roundels to Byzantine cushion capitals and interlaces, to a Greek mask worked into an array of acanthus leaves.*

ABOVE AND LEFT: *The stone room
was Allen Stem's last Summit Avenue
commission. Placed at the rear of the
house, its fine plaster and masonry work is
a perfect complement to the wood carving
and casework of the great hall that leads to
it. The stone on the walls is a variegated
Winona dolomite that accepts a polish,
creating a semblance of Italian marble
at a fraction of the cost.* OPPOSITE:
*Many of the imported historic rooms have
muted colors, highlighted only by scenic or
still-life vignettes and gilt moldings. Time
and atmosphere have dulled and blotched
the original colors, but the patinas of the
original finishes have been preserved as part
of their antique value.*

ABOVE AND LEFT: *The design of elaborate late-19th-century wood carving was commonly a joint venture of architect and artisan, the architect providing the general style or array of styles and the artisan working out the details. Many architectural carvers were trained as sculptors; carving was their day job. The snakelike grapevines below the capital to the right were probably a carver's invention.*

OPPOSITE: *Executing the work required an ever-present assistant to keep sharp knives and chisels in hand. A complex, high-relief panel such as this might have required a dozen different tools.*

by Bette Hammel

S ince 1874, a whole lot of living has gone on at 649 Summit Avenue. Its parade of early owners inevitably changed the floor plan of this French Second Empire-style residence— the only surviving example on Summit—at one point dividing the single-family home into five apartments.

The first owner, real-estate agent and investor Albert George Manson, wanted an imposing structure on the hill. The architect is unknown, but it must have been a master builder who created this fashionable house of creamy white brick, three dormers, corner tower, decorative brackets, and wrought-iron cresting at the roofline. Its Second Empire style is, according to historian Ernest Sandeen, generally Italianate but for the hipped, French (or mansard) roof named for its originator, François Mansart. At least five other homes of the style, modeled after Georges-Eugène Haussmann's opulent rebuilding of Paris under Napoleon III, graced the avenue in the Victorian era.

After a succession of owners, funeral directors John Kessler and Thomas Maguire acquired the house in 1919 and built a circular driveway to accommodate the funeral home they planned to open there. The neighbors objected to having cadavers nearby and took their case all the way to the Minnesota Supreme Court. The court decided for the com- plainants—the city's resplendent avenue should be reserved for the living. The neighbors settled down when yet another owner moved in.

Since creation of the Historic Hill District on the National Register in 1976, the home's architecture has been relatively stable. Former U.S. Senator David Durenburger and his wife, Susan Foote, a retired university professor, bought the property in 1999. "Growing up in San Francisco, I already had a weakness for Victorian houses," says Susan. Senator Durenburger, recalling their time at 649, says, "I en-

OPPOSITE: *In keeping with the historic French character of this 649 Summit house, Stuart MacDonald of MacDonald and Mack Architects designed a new side entrance and terrace overlooking the garden. Painted dark gray over wood framing, the expansion added a major feature to the 1874 house.* ABOVE: *This only surviving French Second Empire-style house on the avenue originally was built for real-estate agent and investor A. G. Manson.*

joyed the uniqueness of the history." And with a chuckle: "Here I was, a newly retired U.S. Senator, living in a former funeral parlor with a need to remove a path for the hearses."

The couple found the house had not lost its character, despite the need for exterior changes due to renovations made in 1989. First they replaced the circular drive with a straightforward, side driveway. They shored up the front porch. And they hired architects Stuart MacDonald (MacDonald and Mack Architects) to build a side entrance and small terrace overlooking the large, new, side garden they installed. After enjoying the home for five years, they sold it in 2004 to another professional couple—Jessica Stoltenberg, a corporate communications consultant, and her husband, physician Phillip Stoltenberg.

The Stoltenbergs admired the home for its elegant style, especially the long curving front porch, mansard roof, and fluted columns. They appreciated the significant improvements—including air-conditioning—made by the previous owners. "We love being caretakers of these old houses," they say. Working with Keri Olson of KOR Interior Design, Jessica soon began redecorating in the style of the period.

The small scale of the rooms especially appealed to the Stoltenbergs. For the entry, which is larger, they chose a soft, "anaglyptic," gold-covered, textured wallpaper with a layered scroll design, similar to European wall coverings of the 1800s. They brightened the ceiling with a tone-on-tone trompe l'oeil with gold-leaf detail and restored the original butternut flooring. In the entry alcove, a leaded-glass transom window studded with gemstones adds color above the previously existing, large, rectangular bay window. To the right (upon entry) is the original butternut stairway complete with original lamp-topped newel post.

Jessica and Phillip chose antique furnishings—for example, a beautiful marquetry entry table—specifically for their Second Empire home. "We like a mix of art and antiques," says Jessica. To the left of the entry is a sitting room, the "Blue Lady," so-named for its art and feminine motif. Thanks to the original builder, the home's many windows bring in natural light, enhancing its beauty.

Jessica used another leaded-glass enhancement, featuring an Art Nouveau-style floral design with translucent stone, for the front window. The dining room, according to designer Olson, is "a historic jewel box." The gold theme of the entry continues on its walls; the ceiling has been backdated with the new plasterwork of a Russian master craftsman. The original fireplace gleams with blue-tile surround; soft, slate-blue "ball gown" draperies with organza embroidery inset frame the windows. Illuminating the room are 19th-century French Empire sconces of ebonized brass with ormolu brackets. This room merited a 2009 ASID MN award for its distinctive design.

A second sitting room is now a cozy family room for modern living, with TV and family memorabilia—such as athletic awards (horse shows and football) and photos—on one wall and books on another. The space leads to the side entry and terrace overlooking the garden. "This is where we unwind and relax," says Jessica. The kitchen, remodeled in 1989, has birch cabinets, proper lighting, up-to-date appliances, and a breakfast area.

Upstairs is the best-known room of the house, recognized for its use as Senator Durenburger's office. The Stoltenbergs have retained its U.S. Capitol-themed wallpaper, extra-large antique desk, and green lampshade. Phillip uses it as an office now.

The owners must soon face replacement of the old mansard shingles, but Jessica says they know "living in old houses requires constant repair and updating." Meanwhile the American flag on the front porch waves as if the third-oldest home on the grandest street in St. Paul were announcing, "I'm proud to be here still."

PREVIOUS PAGE: *The dining room, considered a "jewel" of interior design, won a 2009 ASID MN award of distinction for designer Keri Olson. The French theme carries through with 19th-century sconces of ebonized brass with ormolu brackets. Slate-blue "ball gown" draperies, with organza embroidery inset, grace the windows.*

OPPOSITE: *The Stoltenbergs bought 649 in 2004 from former U.S. Senator David Durenburger and his wife, Susan Foote, a retired University of Minnesota professor. The senator's hand-carved antique desk still fills the space of the second-floor office, where the owners have also retained the U.S. Capitol-themed wallpaper.*

OPPOSITE, TOP LEFT: *The interior rooms are intimate in scale, while the larger entry features a soft, gold-covered wall covering with layered finish and highlighted scroll design.* OPPOSITE, TOP RIGHT: *The original butternut stairway, complete with original lamp-topped newel post, leads to the second-floor bedrooms and office.* OPPOSITE, BOTTOM: *The feminine mystique of the painting over the mantel inspired the name "Blue Lady" for the living room (originally the parlor). A leaded-glass addition to the front window (upper left) features a floral design of translucent stone.*

ABOVE: *A cozy family room, where the family gathers to relax, read, and watch TV, replaces the second "sitting" room. The space provides easy access to the terrace and garden, where the Stoltenbergs also like to unwind.* RIGHT: *The dining room's original fireplace, with blue-tile surround, anchors the elegant space. An antique bench is tucked in front of the fireplace.*

by Bette Hammel

The picturesque Queen Anne Victorian known as the Thurston house stands out at 495 Summit Avenue for its use of color, notably dark teal and cream on the wood trim that frames its vertical windows.

Built in 1881–82, the home's entire exterior was originally of the red brick that is characteristic of early Queen Anne style, also known for its verandas and balconies, grouped windows, gabled roofs, and varied ornamentation. The use of vibrant colors later brightened these large, popular homes from San Francisco to Cape May.

When owners Sheila and James Moar bought the home in 1983 and realized its brick façade had been painted white, they immediately began sandblasting the brick to its original rosy red. In choosing colors for the trim, they consulted architect and member of the St. Paul Historic Preservation Commission Tom Zahn. After examining period wallpapers from the 1930s for appropriate color inspiration, they selected complementary shades including a light aqua for the gabled roofs, to simulate weathering copper. The overall result? "The way the windows are now outlined adds vitality to the street," Sheila says.

At the time this multi-gabled, ornamented house was built, Summit Avenue already held appeal for successful businessmen such as Cyrus B. Thurston and his wife, Mary, who envisioned grand plans for their home. Architect Denslow W. Millard, recently from Illinois, designed the house, apparently in his first St. Paul commission. Thurston was a dealer in carriages and agricultural implements and later ran a cold-storage warehouse near Seven Corners. Daughter Mary married architect Clarence Johnston in 1885.

The Moars chose this Victorian house for its southern exposure and prominent site on the corner of Mackubin Street and Summit, a lot and a half featuring a layered stone wall, green grass, and flowers. It is one of few Summit properties with the original date carved into a dormered gable. A National Trust for Historic Preservation plaque at the covered entry announces that this residence is part of St. Paul's Historic Hill District. The original porch was removed before the Moars acquired the property.

One can imagine the horse-drawn carriages of an earlier day bringing people up and down the avenue, dropping passengers at a side entrance to 495. Sheila put to advantage what was once a roof over what she surmises was an entry and had it rebuilt as an attractive narrow balcony overlooking the side yard and street.

OPPOSITE: *"Playful and colorful" describes the exterior of this 1881 Victorian built for businessman Cyrus F. Thurston. Owners Sheila and James Moar returned the white-painted façade to its original rosy brick, with painted aqua trim.* ABOVE: *Americans love ornamented Victorians with turrets, towers, and gables like this one containing even the street address.* NEXT PAGE: *Leaded-glass windows in a bay overlooking the solid oak staircase brighten the entry and its original cherry, oak, and mahogany parquet floor.*

Much of the original interior of the home—especially its handsome woodwork and carved fireplaces—has been saved. Upon entering through a set of heavy, carved-wood doors, the visitor steps into a wide entry hall featuring four leaded-glass windows set into a bay, to bring in the natural light. Tall, vertical, double-hung, leaded-glass windows enhance all the main-floor and side rooms but the dining room, which features two stained-glass windows in lavenders and greens. Adding to the home's Victorian character are a solid oak staircase in the front hallway and an oak fireplace surround of handmade, Craftsman-style, green tiles. Fronting the fireplace opening is an ornate cover of decorative metal colored to resemble wood. There are three other wood-burning fireplaces on the first floor and another on the second.

Sheila values the welcoming way the main-floor rooms flow one into another—living room to library to dining room. The 12-foot-high ceilings add to the general feeling of openness. In the living room, earlier the "drawing room," one of the four previous owners had removed a fireplace; later a 4-foot by 12-foot mirror of Bavarian glass was installed. Sheila had the ceiling painted blue, pink, and lavender to approximate Monet's painting *The Lilies*. An Asian, Art Deco carpet in lavender hues completes the more intimate space.

ABOVE, LEFT: *Cut-glass windows brighten the entryway on the west side of the house, facing Mackubin Street.* ABOVE, RIGHT AND OPPOSITE, TOP: *Above the hand-carved fireplace in the dining room is a colorful fan from Hong Kong. Owner Sheila Moar mixes Asian art and artifacts with contemporary objects throughout the home. The vintage chandelier of colored art glass and brass is by Quoizel, a 1930s associate of Tiffany.* OPPOSITE, BOTTOM RIGHT AND LEFT: *Four wood-burning fireplaces remain operative. The entry fireplace includes a handmade, Craftsman-style, green-tile hearth.*

The rectangular library, with mahogany paneling and built-in bookcases, features an unusual fireplace surround. Its rows of hand-painted tiles depict the stories of Charles Dickens, delighting both children and adults of the neighborhood. The original cherry, oak, and mahogany parquet floors of the library extend through the main floor.

In the dining room is a vintage chandelier of colored art glass and brass by Quoizel, a 1930s associate of Tiffany. Sheila collects Asian artifacts and antiques and mixes them with contemporary pieces. Above the hand-carved fireplace, she has placed a colorful fan depicting scenes from Hong Kong.

Like many other owners of vintage homes, the Moars have completely renovated their kitchen despite earlier remodeling efforts. Early in their ownership, they outfitted the kitchen with modern appliances, a wood island, and white Corian® and granite countertops. They also exposed an original brick wall behind the new oven. To lighten the north-facing space, they have painted the walls in Tuscan yellow and terra-cotta, removed a wall, and installed a row of new windows to reveal a landscaped backyard patio and garden. And they remodeled a room off the kitchen as a combination family room and office.

St. Paul owes much to residents like the Moars, who have helped to preserve homes along the most famous Victorian boulevard in America.

OPPOSITE, LEFT: *The dining-room furniture includes antiques such as this handsome chest and built-in mirror.*

OPPOSITE, RIGHT: *The intricate wood carving on the library fireplace surround is the handiwork of craftsmen in a house retaining much of its original finishes, walls, floors, and windows.* ABOVE: *Thanks to D. W. Millard, who made the plans, the Moars loved this house at first glance for its room flow. From a corner of the library, one can easily see to the dining room.*

RIGHT: *Captivating hand-painted tiles in the library's fireplace surround depict the stories of Charles Dickens, delighting neighbors and friends.*

452 LAUREL AVENUE   *by Melinda Nelson*

Graced by the presence of the Cathedral of Saint Paul and dotted with romantic street names such as Arundel, Iglehart, and Ashland, the Cathedral Hill neighborhood retains much of its original storybook charm. On Laurel Avenue, a stone's throw from the St. Paul Curling Club, a tiny, white house with a blue door sits squarely in the middle of a lush, green lawn. Known to historians as the William W. Howard House, the home is more commonly referred to as "the dollhouse" by neighbors and passersby, who appreciate its diminutive stature and charming details.

Howard was a clerk for the St. Paul, Minneapolis, and Manitoba Railway. He and his wife, Ella, commissioned Charles E. Plummer to build their home, which was completed in 1884 for $3,000. That same year, Plummer built a home at 472 Laurel for C. G. Kolff, a colleague of Howard. The builder was likely inspired by *Cottage and Villa Architecture*, a pattern book published in 1878 with "plans, elevations, sections, and details of low-priced, medium, and first-class cottages, villas, farm houses, and country seats."

Howard's house is a delightful iteration of the Stick-Eastlake style, with steep-pitched roofs, overhanging eaves, exposed trusses, narrow lap siding, horizontal windows, and decorative wood ornamentation. Charles Locke Eastlake (1836–1906) was a British architect, furniture designer, and devotee of William Morris. An advocate of the Arts and Crafts movement, Eastlake believed that furnishings and accessories should be made by hand or by machine workers who took pride in their work. His book *Hints on Household Taste in Furniture, Upholstery, and Other Details* was published in 1872 and became so popular that it was reprinted six times within 11 years.

OPPOSITE: *Roddie Turner's 1884 Stick-Eastlake-style cottage was likely built from a pattern book.*
ABOVE: *The diminutive foyer offers a welcome message and a stoup filled with holy water.*

If every home has a story and each homeowner writes a new chapter, Roddie Turner was destined to own the dollhouse on Laurel Avenue. A gifted designer, stylist, and cook, Turner shares Eastlake's passion for the handmade. "I adore old things, and I spent many years collecting antiques, handmade objects, religious reliquaries, heart-shaped rocks, sparkling minerals, and other treasures," she says. "I love using what I have and retrofitting things for a new purpose, like using French shutters to make a closet door or displaying a roll of music from an old player piano as a piece of art."

Turner bought the Howard house in October 2008 as the result of events culminating in what she calls "a lovely happenstance." As the youngest of her four children was finishing high school, she found herself looking for a new nest. On one of her frequent bike rides through Cathedral Hill, she saw a "for sale" sign on the dollhouse. She called her realtor, who agreed that the home was "cute as a bug" but cautioned Turner that the interior was a little eccentric.

PREVIOUS PAGES: *Turner painted the original fireplace a soft gray to complement her grandmother's purple velvet chairs.*

OPPOSITE: *Turner loves mixing antiques with found objects, such as a roll of player-piano music with the lyrics "Flying with flowing sail over the summer sea . . . homeward bound was she."*

As soon as Turner stepped across the threshold, she knew the home was meant to be hers: "It was a totally perfect space for me, with everything I wanted, including a good-sized kitchen, a dining room for entertaining, and a garden." Undaunted by the awkward foyer and other challenges, she was energized by the opportunity to put her own imprimatur on the house. "I'm really fortunate in that I've always lived in great houses, full of wonderful possibilities, and I've been able to tinker with each one of them," she says. "But this is the first house that's just mine, which is really significant. I was married early, so I never lived on my own, never had a single-girl apartment. This house gave me the chance to define a new life for myself."

Armed with the vision of a small Scandinavian cottage painted in shades of gray, champagne, and cream, Turner worked her magic on every room. She removed remnants of outdated renovation projects including a clunky center island and a desk hutch in the kitchen

Down with pretense, sham, aesthetic quackery; up with honesty, sincerity.

—CHARLES LOCKE EASTLAKE, 1870

and rigorously edited her collection of antiques, art, and found objects to fit her new space.

Turner also turned her designer's eye on the gardens. Inspired by the all-white garden at Sissinghurst, in Kent, England, she planted the flowerbeds with white Annabelle and Limelight hydrangeas, white flowering hosta, white astilbe, white peonies, white violets, white roses, and white clematis, which she says is "just luminous against the house." After commissioning a friend of her daughter to build a simple wood fence, Turner and her children and their friends spent a summer day staining and installing the fence. Afterward, they all sat down to enjoy one of Turner's legendary gourmet dinners. "It was one of my happiest days. It was just perfect—family, food, and creativity. That's the trifecta."

A designer's work is never done, so Turner continues to work her magic throughout the house. She recently replaced 144 Eastlake-style spindles in the railing of the upstairs porch, and she's having custom molding installed in the parlor to match the molding in the living room. She is also eyeing a piece of marble in her garage, thinking about using it to create a butler's pantry in a closet in the kitchen.

Sitting at the kitchen table, planning the menu for an upcoming wedding, Turner reflects on the journey that led her to the door of the dollhouse. "For some people, food simply provides fuel, and houses provide shelter, but I'm not one of them. I feel lucky to live in such a special house and to be able to put my stamp on it," she says. "When I come home at the end of the day, the house just shimmers."

OPPOSITE: *The Murano glass chandelier has illuminated several of Turner's previous homes. The antique dining-room table belonged to Turner's grandmother, and the chairs were a gift from Turner's children. She found the oil painting at an artist's studio in the Northrup King Building in Minneapolis.* ABOVE AND RIGHT: *Turner gave the kitchen a simple facelift with a mix of industrial and rustic design elements. She repainted existing cabinets a charcoal color, added subway tiles and new hardware, and removed a clunky center island to make room for a handmade farm table and white chairs. She finished the space with an ivory antique hutch that she's owned for years, wire baskets, antique glass, and a simple industrial-inspired chandelier.*

OPPOSITE, TOP LEFT: *The cottage's steep-pitched roofs, narrow lap siding, and decorative balconet ornamentation are hallmarks of the Stick-Eastlake style.* OPPOSITE, TOP RIGHT AND BOTTOM: *Turner used her simple yet sophisticated design aesthetic to create an outdoor dining room.* ABOVE: *Turner, a professional cook, loves hosting dinner parties on her patio. The designer's gardens are an homage to the all-white gardens at Sissinghurst, in Kent, England. Inspired by Vita Sackville-West, Turner planted white varieties of Annabelle and Limelight hydrangeas, flowering hostas, astilbe, peonies, violets, roses, and clematis, which she says are "just luminous against the house."* RIGHT: *Seen through Turner's eyes, rust and chipped enamel are exquisite forms of patina.*

F rederick and Lucy Driscoll's brick and brownstone mansion attracted national attention soon after its completion. Featured in East Coast art critic George Sheldon's lavish *Artistic Country Seats*, it stood shoulder to shoulder with the landmark work of both Peabody & Stearns and McKim, Mead and White. St. Paul journalists called it one of "the conspicuous ornaments of Summit Avenue," "the most sumptuous of its stately homes," and "the handsomest residences in St. Paul."

Its architect, William H. Willcox, was unique among his St. Paul peers for his arrival with impressive portfolio already in hand. Among his accomplishments were churches in New York City and Chicago—and the Nebraska State Capitol in Lincoln. Built in 1884, the Driscoll house was Willcox's first major residential project in St. Paul.

That same year, Willcox published *Hints to Those Who Propose to Build*. This pamphlet was both an advertisement of his work and a paean to functionality, unity, and harmony in architecture. His largest commissions in St. Paul—Park Congregational Church, the original building for Macalester College, and the Bank of Minnesota—drew instant praise for those qualities. All went up between 1883 and 1886, just before Willcox joined Clarence Johnston in the most successful partnership of the great 1880s building boom. All three structures have disappeared over the last 70 years.

The modern eye struggles to find evidence of Willcox following his own principles in the multiple window shapes and sizes, picturesque roofline, and variegated materials of the Driscoll house. He filled out the building permits himself, scrawling across the line item for dimensions: "Irregular, must refer to plans." Duluth brownstone belt courses and a terra-cotta frieze tie the house together horizontally, but they must leap over an amazing sequence of projecting towers, window bays, and dormers. A walk-through reveals an array of distinct spaces, each designed for a specific purpose. The plan shows Willcox's genius—these unique spaces fan out from a central hall, treating the entrant in a single sweep of the eye to glimpses of the architectural riches beyond.

OPPOSITE: *The Driscoll—Weyerhaeuser house today retains its distinctive configuration of pressed red brick, Duluth brownstone, and terra-cotta. The degree of ornamental masonry detail is unusual even for Summit Avenue.* ABOVE: *Frederick and Lucy Driscoll's house looked like this shortly after completion. Note Willcox's original elaborate porch and the picturesque skyline of witch's hat, molded chimneys, and ornamental gables.*

Built in 1884, the Driscoll residence rose in three months, the standard duration for Summit Avenue's grand homes until construction of the James J. Hill house, a few houses to the east, turned months into years. Pre-Civil War homes were fair game for replacement by bigger and more stylish residences, just as the replacements would become vulnerable to waning Victorian taste after World War I. Whatever their size or magnificence, their survival depended on little more than the whims and aspirations of their owners—to adapt historic building stock or to embrace current stylistic trends and modern floor plans.

OPPOSITE: *For the 2001 ASID MN Showcase Home Tour, interior designer Brandi Hagen and her team of experts masterfully recreated the great hall and upstairs landing to include exquisite window treatments, fabrics, upholstery, and hand-woven rugs in regal shades.* ABOVE: *The pargework ceiling treatment in the upstairs landing is an outstanding original feature of the house brought to life with a touch of color.* RIGHT: *The grand staircase, with authentic iron railings, meets the checker-board marble floor to anchor the faux-treated walls, painted to resemble limestone.*

At the time he built his Summit Avenue house, Frederick Driscoll (1833–1907) was on the brink of achieving a national reputation greater than that of his architect. General manager of the *St. Paul Press* and its successor, the *St. Paul Pioneer Press*, from 1863, he was an active Republican and "militant Minnesotan" with well-known outbursts that "took on a lurid sunset crimson" at the frequent political chicanery of his era. He was also a founder of the Associated Press, an early advocate of typesetting machines, and a national leader in promoting and adjudicating arbitration between publishers and typographers.

Widowed in 1880, Driscoll took a new bride, Lucy Norris Styles, in 1882. That made their house on Summit Avenue—like the Doty house on Portland—a place for a fresh beginning, albeit with three nearly grown sons. The Driscoll boys left—one by one—until Fred and Lucy themselves left for smaller quarters in 1892, selling the house to lumberman Frederick Weyerhaeuser.

Few changes to the house occurred through the remainder of Weyerhaeuser's life. On his death in 1914, his eldest son, Rudolph M. Weyerhaeuser, returned to St. Paul from his lumber operations in Cloquet, Minnesota, and took possession. The following year Rudolph called on Emmanuel L. Masqueray, architect of the Cathedral of Saint Paul, to refurbish and in some cases reconstruct the parts of the home most conspicuously out of date.

OPPOSITE: *Once surrounded by houses of equal Victorian exuberance, the Driscoll house has survived as one of the "grand old dames" of Summit Avenue. Masqueray's remodeling of the entry and the modern porte cochere have not compromised its high-flying Queen Anne style.* ABOVE: *ASID MN designers Bruce Kading and Brian Ellingson brought updated traditional furniture and accessories in a neutral palette to the design of the stately walnut-paneled living room and library.* RIGHT: *Decorative painter Brian Schindlbeck created the intricately patterned hand-stained latticework floor punctuated by a compass motif in the center of each square.*

OPPOSITE: *A team of ASID MN interior designers including Pat Manning-Hanson, Shelley Bowman, Leila Lake, Debbie Miller, and Mary Kassner reinvented the dining room with celadon-colored walls and ormolu-styled treatment over the hand-carved pilasters flanking the picture window.* BELOW: *For the dining-room fireplace, Masqueray put aside his canon of simplicity for a built-up ceiling cove and carved wall panels reaching ten feet. The 2001 showcase designers envisioned the patina effect.*

At a cost of $15,000 ($300,000 in curent dollars), Masqueray added the most fashionable remodeling of the day, a rear porch topped with a sleeping porch. He also replaced the elaborately spindled front porch with a simple Neoclassical portico and remodeled the dining-room wing. Those remodelings were mentioned in the building permit and in published building news. But his hand is evident everywhere—in the wrought-iron railings, picture-frame wall moldings, and piers announcing the transition from one room to another. In each case, unmistakably French touches cover or obliterate the English influence of Willcox's work.

On the outside, Masqueray enhanced his new entry with an Art Nouveau railing, removed a second-floor balcony out of harmony with the new portico below, and refashioned the exterior ornament outside the old dining room to show off the transformation within.

Rudolph and Louise Lindeke Weyerhaeuser fled to Cloquet during the remodeling, returning to enjoy their "new" house until Rudolph's death in 1946 and Louise's in the early 1950s. Then the house went the way of many of the grand old Summit Avenue manors, to a succession of institutional tenants—first to the Indianhead Council of the Boy Scouts of America and then to the Epiphany House of Prayer.

After returning to private ownership just before the new century, the house became a St. Paul ASID MN Showcase Home in 2001. The only significant exterior alteration in modern times is a sensitively designed porte cochere at the west end. The house carries the stamp of yet a third century's designers—like Masqueray, sensitive to the architectural fabric but making a pointedly modern signature.

One of the finest examples of St. Paul's historic architecture is Laurel Terrace, the 1887 row house dubbed "Riley's Row" by journalists for its first owner, William C. Riley. Today it is known as Riley Row. Architects Willcox and Johnston were just starting their partnership, loaded with fresh ideas. Their joint creation of the row house was a dramatic achievement—a design of strength, flair, and romance.

Built of redstone and red pressed brick, with granite on the first-floor columns, the façade of the three-story Romanesque Revival structure is distinctive on all three levels. First designed as seven townhouses in one block, the row house was later divided for other use (such as apartments) for various homeowners. Broad sweeping arches differentiate the living units, each marked by a colorful sunburst and topped with matching gables. Myriad gargoyles, griffins, nymphs, cupids, and floral ornaments are carved into the sculptural stone.

OPPOSITE: *Known as one of the finest Victorian row houses in America, Laurel Terrace earned a national reputation for architects Willcox and Johnston early in their partnership. With sculpted redstone façade stretching a full block, the building was originally seven townhouses, later divided into apartments.* ABOVE: *William Willcox often used floral motifs such as this carved portion of a capital at Laurel Terrace.*

When new owners bought No. 286 in 1983, they decided to return it to its original, single-family-townhouse state. They liked the neighborhood and were intrigued with the turret and the unusual façade of the row house. Gradually they renovated their space, widening the rooms by narrowing the stairway and building bookcases for their extensive library. In the pleasant living room, the original fireplace still burns wood, the ceiling retains its early dentiling, and a French door with divided-light windows brightens the living room and connected dining room. Because the owners also enjoy gardening, they created a shared courtyard garden in back that winds through the narrow space between buildings.

More recent is the installation of a new entry door featuring the leaves of the gingko tree on the Laurel Avenue boulevard in a wrought-iron design by metalworkers John Yust and Chris Rand. AIA architect Yust of St. Paul oversaw the renovation of 286.

The Laurel Terrace turret is a neighborhood landmark, its cone-shaped "Roman" tower topped with dormers and finials thrusting into the sky. Perhaps the charm of Riley Row also persuaded F. Scott Fitzgerald's maternal grandmother, Louisa Allen McQuillan, to establish residence in another townhouse there. She (and later Scott's parents) kept an extra bedroom for Scott, who lived there from 1908 to 1909.

The owners of 286 agree that Riley Row, known as one of the finest Victorian row houses in the United States, is indeed a unique place to live, and they are happy that part of it is solely their own. As for the carved creatures on their home's exterior stone arch, they say they love their lizards—one of the many animated ornamental features of the exterior façade.

OPPOSITE, TOP LEFT: *Leafy petals surround this smiling cherub, one of a variety of faces, gargoyles, nymphs, elves, mascaron, and floral ornaments on the Laurel Terrace façade.* OPPOSITE, BOTTOM RIGHT: *This portion of archway typifies the carved images that give the Romanesque Revival structure its singular appearance—note the reptilian motif clinging to the haunch of the arch.* ABOVE: *Heralding the neighborhood is an Old World, cone-shaped turret clad with Gothic dormers and finials thrusting to the sky.* RIGHT: *A colorful sunburst design marks the entrance of each dwelling, showing just what skilled 1880s craftsmen could do.*

OPPOSITE: *The current owners of 286 Laurel Terrace converted what was an apartment into the original townhouse form. The living room retains its original wood-burning fireplace, dentil molding, divided-light windows, and French doors.*

RIGHT: *A beautiful courtyard garden winds around the back of the row house, which includes a patio for dining outdoors.*

BELOW, LEFT: *In the light-filled dining room, the owners saved the original mantel and golden yellow tiles of the fireplace surround. They also installed a large modern window to overlook their garden.*

BELOW, RIGHT: *A 21st-century entry door greets visitors to this historic residence. Metalworker Chris Rand created a wrought-iron screen featuring the leaves of the gingko tree on Laurel Boulevard. AIA architect John Yust oversaw the renovation.*

F rom morning until dusk, an American flag waves from the porch of the house at 767 Goodrich Avenue. Every evening, Becky Diekmann takes down the flag and rolls it up for safekeeping until the next day. Becky and her husband, Paul, have owned their home for 12 years, but stars and stripes have flown over the house since 1888, when it was built for William Gardner White.

White was a native of Massachusetts and a descendant of Elder John White, a charter member of the Massachusetts Bay Colony. His great-grandfather Gardner Preston was a Minuteman who fought in the American Revolution. After White graduated from Harvard Law School in 1874, he practiced in Springfield, Illinois, for three years and then ventured west to St. Paul, where he became a cofounder of the National Investment Company.

In 1888 White and his wife, Carolyn E. Hall, commissioned the architectural firm of Willcox and Johnston to design a home for themselves and their three children—Marion, Edwin, and William. Built at a cost of $7,000, the turreted Queen Anne Victorian mansion features shingle siding, leaded bay windows, a wrought-iron fence, and a Neoclassical front porch with five columns.

When White died in 1919, his son Edwin and his wife, Anne Turney White, inherited the home. Edwin, a graduate of Yale, was an investment banker and the founder of Edwin White and Company. Anne and her friends Elizabeth Ames Jackson and Elizabeth Crunden Skinner established the Junior League of St. Paul. Edwin served on several boards, including that of Northwest Airlines, where he enthusiastically embraced the future of aviation. He was equally passionate about fishing, hunting with his great-great-great grandfather's deer rifle, and good manners.

When the White children were growing up, Edwin wrote a letter to Emily Post. After complimenting her on a recent article, he suggested several "other little table tricks [that] are equally important. To begin—I think it most civilized and genial for the family to gather in the living room five or ten minutes before the hour appointed for dinner. It's distressing to send a maid upstairs to hunt up the slow members of the clan or for the punctual parent to whistle upstairs for the late comers."

LEFT: *William White commissioned the architectural firm of Willcox and Johnston to design this Queen Anne Victorian mansion in 1888.* ABOVE: *The ornate, carved woodwork was inspired by Johnston's design.*

Anne White had a passion and a talent for interior design. In an article entitled "The Home of the North," Virginia Safford, columnist for the *Minneapolis Star and Tribune*, wrote that Anne's "fine sense of color is apparent in everything she has touched . . . She seems to have been able to select the things that will endure—things that will be as charming tomorrow as they are today." Calling the drawing room "unforgettable," Safford noted the pale blue walls,

the graceful sofa and chairs upholstered in "rich tan velvet," lamps with silver bases, a pair of dark-blue glass jars, "a growing plant," and even a polar-bear skin, concluding, "Everything is in harmony yet gives no impression of having been created to indulge any faddy notions."

More than half a century later, in a curious twist of design destiny, Becky and Paul painted those same walls blue. "We thought long and hard about the color and finally decided on Aegean blue," says Paul. Just as Anne White did, Becky filled the room with a harmonious mix of antique furniture, including a graceful chaise longue upholstered in tan burlap, vintage silver, moss-covered statuary, and various forms of taxidermy. "Becky has a great eye," says Tommy Brandt, designer and friend of the Diekmanns. "She's always coming home with old leather-bound books, pieces of coral, and other soulful stuff. Though they're all inanimate objects, they hit you in your heart."

When the Diekmanns bought the William G. White House, they were expecting their sixth child. The family had been living on Holly Avenue in the Cathedral Hill neighborhood with "five kids, one dog, a huge oak tree, and a small lot," explains Paul. "Because our home was in a historic district, we couldn't enlarge the garage to fit an eight-passenger vehicle, so we had to find a bigger house."

The previous owners, Dick and Nancy Nicholson, restored several rooms in the house, but the third floor required a total renovation. With the help of designer and friend Shari Wilsey, the Diekmanns gutted and rebuilt the third floor, then furnished the house with their signature mix of art, antiques, and found objects.

Becky often accompanies Paul, an orthopedic surgeon, when he attends medical conferences across the United States. They especially enjoy visiting Atlanta and New Orleans, where they've become friends with several antique dealers. On one trip to Atlanta, they found an opulent gilded frame from an Italian convent. Fitted with a mirror, it now occupies pride of place in the dining room, near one of Paul's most cherished possessions, a 15th-century illuminated antiphon manuscript from Italy. In the French Quarter of New Orleans, the Diekmanns found a Georgian bowfront dresser and an English clock from 1808, which now chimes the hour from its post in the living room. Across the room, a World War I parade helmet, jauntily placed by Tommy, perches on the head of a statue.

Since Shari introduced Tommy Brandt to the Diekmanns five years ago, he has become a beloved member of the family. When he's not rearranging furniture and styling Becky's treasures into quirky vignettes layered with whimsy, faith, and humor, Brandt helps her take care of the gardens and ready the house for holidays, family gatherings, and dinner parties. "Home is a respite from the world, so it can't be chaotic," says Brandt. "Becky and Paul's house is bohemian, comfortable, and alive, both physically and spiritually. I just help them make it more beautiful."

OPPOSITE: *The ceiling is painted with scenes from a memorable family trip to Italy. St. Nicholas twirls a parasol, courtesy of inimitable designer Tommy Brandt.* RIGHT: *A framed, Italian illuminated antiphon manuscript from the 15th century, one of Paul's most cherished possessions, hangs above one of the home's original fireplaces.* BELOW, LEFT: *The library features a wealth of carved detail and leaded windows. Shari Wilsey, designer and family friend, gave Paul the antique, amber-glass, medicinal bottles.* BELOW, RIGHT: *In 1888, the White home, designed by Willcox and Johnston with abundant woodwork, leaded windows, and other luxurious details, cost $7,000 to build. Faith, history, and an appreciation for nature infuse every room in the Diekmann home.*

PREVIOUS PAGES: *Nearly a century after Anne White painted the walls of the living room pale blue, the Diekmanns chose a similar shade for their walls. "We thought long and hard about the color and finally decided on Aegean blue," says Paul.* THIS PAGE: *Designer Tommy Brandt often stops by to style Becky's treasures into vignettes, help with the gardens, and ready the house for parties and other events: "Becky and I both love bringing organic things into a room, anything living—statuary covered in moss, corkscrew willow branches, and other greenery."* OPPOSITE: *Blue is a perfect backdrop for the Diekmanns' collection of religious paintings, candelabra, statuary, gilt-framed mirrors, seashells, and objets d'art. "Becky has a great eye," says Brandt. "She's always coming home with old leather-bound books, pieces of coral, and other soulful stuff. Though they're all inanimate objects, they hit you in your heart."* FOLLOWING PAGES: *The Diekmanns have furnished their home with English, French, Italian, and Chinese art and antiques from their favorite shops in St. Paul, Minneapolis, the French Quarter of New Orleans, and Atlanta.*

DIDRIK OMEYER HOUSE

by Dave Kenney

The next time you need a little cheering up, take a stroll down the 800 block of Goodrich Avenue in St. Paul's Crocus Hill neighborhood. There, on the south side of the street, you'll find a house capable of coaxing giggles of delight. The residence at 808 Goodrich is a carnival of Victorian excess, the architectural equivalent of strawberry shortcake. Just try to walk by without smiling.

The house is the work of Didrik Omeyer and Martin Thori, a pair of Norwegian-born architects who designed some of St. Paul's most effusive Queen Anne homes. Completed in 1889, the house apparently sat empty for at least a year while Omeyer tried to find a buyer. For most of

OPPOSITE: *From the half-moon window nestled in the main gable to the procession of hand-turned spindles lining the porch below, the house at 808 Goodrich is a feast of Victorian ornamentation.* ABOVE: *A fanlike arch creates a playful focal point on the left side of the reconstructed front porch.*

the 1890s it served as the home of local rug and wallpaper merchant Charles O. Rice and his widowed mother, Ruth Anna Rice. After the Rices moved out in 1898, the house welcomed a succession of owners including a Unitarian minister, a wholesale merchant, a physician, and a prominent attorney.

As the years went by, much of the house's ornamentation fell victim to the devastations of time and weather. The cantilevered eave extending beyond the recessed third-floor balcony was removed. Spindles and knobs rotted. Brackets and balusters disappeared. Candy-colored paint bubbled and peeled. The adorable Queen Anne lost its youthful exuberance. By the time it reached its 100th birthday, its playful personality had retreated behind a sheathing of asbestos siding and a nondescript front porch rejecting every Omeyer and Thori extravagance.

In 2000 a young property manager who had grown up in the nearby Desnoyer Park neighborhood decided to take a chance on the faded Victorian. The new owner had developed a fondness for Queen Annes while mowing lawns in Crocus Hill during his teens. He was determined to raise the house's spirits.

The owner started in the attic, which was cluttered with decades of residential detritus. He soon discovered that the room's nine-foot ceiling concealed a 20-foot vault. He removed the false ceiling, opened up the space, and converted what had been a dark and dusty storage area into a sunny and spacious master-bedroom suite. The rejuvenation of Omeyer and Thori's old Queen Anne was underway.

Next came what promised to be the house's most challenging restoration project—the front porch. The owner considered the existing porch "a cut-and-paste job" unworthy of the house's Victorian pedigree. He felt it made a poor first impression. "The house really warranted the original porch," he says. "I made the commitment to start over."

ABOVE, LEFT: *A brawny pineapple finial,
representing hospitality, caps the midpoint
newel of the main staircase.* ABOVE,
RIGHT: *Large central circles surrounded by
jewel-like beading are among the details that
make the stairway's stained-glass windows
unique.* LEFT: *The homeowners' dogs, Bear
and Stella, find a comfortable resting place
in the light-filled stairwell.* OPPOSITE:
*The central staircase restoration, overseen
by Bob Hengelfelt, features more than
75 spindles. Handcrafted and installed by
Stephen Vadnais, the finial, hubs, and
spindles were calibrated on site, then hand-
turned on a simple lathe and positioned
over a two-week period.*

At first he had no idea what the original porch looked like. But then, during a research expedition to the University of Minnesota, he came across an 1893 plan book by Omeyer and Thori titled *Home for All*. On its cover was a line drawing of the house at 808 Goodrich. He now knew what the front porch was supposed to look like. But how to recreate it?

He found the answer to that question in the person of master restoration specialist Bob Hengelfelt. Using the Omeyer and Thori line drawing as a guide, Hengelfelt prepared a new set of porch plans and oversaw the reproduction of all the original woodwork—everything from the colonnettes to the goose-neck railings to the fan-shaped, off-center arch. "He just absolutely nailed every detail," the owner says.

The first-floor interior did not require a front-porch-style overhaul, but it did need a good bit of loving care. The main staircase, just off the front parlor, ranked among the highest priorities. Decades of hard use (the home spent about 40 years as a rooming house) had taken a toll on the stairway's intricate woodwork. About 75 spindles were missing. Again, Bob Hengelfelt came to the rescue. He plucked surviving pieces from the balustrades, and they were reproduced on a lathe. "You have to look real close to tell which ones are original and which ones aren't," the owner says.

Hengelfelt also put considerable time and effort into the recreation of the crown molding that lines the intersection of wall and ceiling on the entire first floor. A previous owner had removed nearly all the original molding, leaving only one section, in the rear office. With that clue in hand, Hengelfelt was able to reproduce Omeyer and Thori's ceiling-hugging friezes and rosettes and give the main floor a proper crowning touch.

The kitchen, located at the rear, posed one final challenge. While not as old as many other parts of the home, it did not meet the standards of the owner's new partner—a woman he describes as a "fantastic cook." The previous owners had added an adjacent breakfast room looking out on the backyard, so there was room to expand. The new owner decided to stretch the kitchen into that space and embark on a complete makeover including modern appliances and granite counters.

Now, after more than a decade of meticulous renovation work, the house at 808 Goodrich has reclaimed much of its turn-of-the-century charm. The owner and his partner enjoy nothing more than sitting on their gingerbread-encrusted front porch and watching smiles come to the faces of neighbors and strangers. The house has that effect on people. It may not be the biggest Queen Anne in St. Paul, but it certainly is one of the most fun to see.

599 SUMMIT AVENUE

by Bette Hammel

For 94 years, F. Scott Fitzgerald has cast a spell over readers both young and old, captivated by his romance with the beautiful Zelda Sayre of Alabama and the wild life they led.

In 1919, after dropping out of Princeton University and serving in the army, the 23-year-old Fitzgerald returned to his parents' rented townhouse at 599 Summit Avenue, determined to win Zelda's love by rewriting his first novel, *The Romantic Egotist*. Confining himself to a small, third-floor bedroom, he wrote madly for three months, pinning up pages on the curtains and crawling over the windowsill for an occasional smoke on the balcony.

The book he so desperately produced—retitled *This Side of Paradise* by his publisher—became a national bestseller for Charles Scribner's Sons in April 1920. Its financial success won him Zelda's hand in marriage and set the stage for the couple's personification of the Jazz Age and decline as members of the "Lost Generation" of 1920s America.

Known as Summit Terrace, the Romanesque Revival structure still slows traffic as curious tourists stop to determine exactly which unit Fitzgerald lived in. Little could architects Clarence Johnston and William Willcox have dreamed the brownstone row house they designed in 1889 would gain such notoriety. The current owners, Mike and Nancy Jones, say passersby have even tried to peek in the front windows. Now the 1972 plaque announcing No. 559's status as a National Historic Landmark causes tourists to stop at the sidewalk.

The townhouse structure complete with turrets, small balconies, roughhewn decoration, and slate roof, contains eight units for single-family occupancy. There is no home-owners' association, according to Nancy, "and we all get along." Most of the current owners have lived in the building for years.

OPPOSITE AND ABOVE: *The brownstone row house known as Summit Terrace is famous as the residence where F. Scott Fitzgerald rewrote his first bestseller—*This Side of Paradise. *A National Historic Landmark, the Romanesque Revival structure designed by Johnston and Willcox encompasses eight single-family units.*

The Joneses bought their unit in 1997, just after their return from Brussels, where Mike was on assignment for 3M. That F. Scott Fitzgerald once lived in the unit had nothing to do with their decision to buy it: "We enjoyed living in an attractive townhouse near the inner city in Brussels, so we decided to find a similar situation here," he says.

The Joneses' collection of antiques fits well into this Victorian setting. Originally, their three-story unit was constructed as a four-bedroom residence with two additional bedrooms in the back for the use of domestic employees. Yet after four successive owners, the unit's room configuration remains the same. The current owners have done their own redecorating,

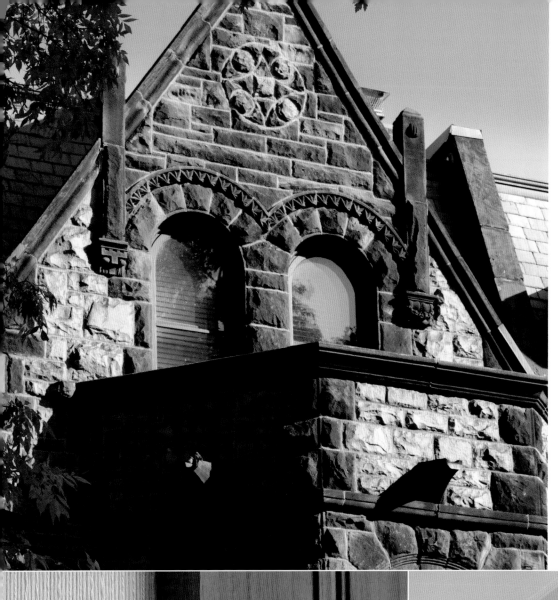

LEFT: *In this top-floor room of his parents' rented townhouse, Fitzgerald wrote madly, determined to win Zelda Sayre with his success. Sometimes he climbed out the window onto the balcony for a smoke. His novel, published in April 1920, was a smash hit.* BELOW, LEFT: *On the third floor at the front is "the writing room," where Scott pinned chapter outlines to the curtains and called through a "speaking tube" to ask his parents for a snack.* This Side of Paradise *set the scene for America's* Roaring Twenties. BELOW, RIGHT: *Thirty-nine steps lead to ample bedrooms, bath, and other spaces on the second and third floors.*

planned for the entire stairway to act as a chimney, funneling hot air up through a cupola to exit the house. Today a fixed skylight brightens the area.

The Joneses call the third-floor study where Fitzgerald wrote "the writing room." Mike designed and built its first-class bookcase; the couple furnished the room further with a roll-top desk and chair. The only original element here is a "speaking tube," through which F. Scott called his parents to request more food. Nevertheless, and despite the fact that the famous writer lived at this address only three months, the story of his beloved and their tormented lives evokes in this home the mystique of that romantic era.

Today the Joneses reminisce about F. Scott Fitzgerald when a current movie or play features his work—and during St. Paul's home-tour season. Nancy enjoys working in her tiny front-yard garden, tending to her window boxes on the second-floor balcony, and hanging out at a local nursery. On non-golfing days, Mike heads for the basement to select tools for his current woodworking effort or to make some wine.

Together the Joneses have recreated a Victorian home, more modest than the larger houses along Summit Avenue, perhaps, but with every bit the charm.

by Melinda Nelson

S t. Paul's Cathedral Hill is home to a tight-knit group of friends who lovingly refer to their city as "St. Small" as they chat over coffee at Nina's, brunch at W. A. Frost, and dinner parties at each other's homes. Bound by decades of shared family history and deep civic pride, they open their homes for concerts, walking tours, and garden tours and wave to bicyclists touring the picturesque streets. In an architectural twist on Monopoly, the friends speak of their neighbors and the architects of their homes in the same breath. "They're redoing a Reed and Stem," they'll say. "She's a member of the Clarence Johnston fan club," or "They just bought the Cass Gilbert on Summit and Farrington."

A century ago, when Johnston, Stem, and Gilbert were designing mansions, their clients were building railroads, running dry-goods emporiums, managing vast sums of money, and providing the legal counsel and other services required by a fast-growing state. When these captains of industry weren't convening in the boardrooms of downtown St. Paul, they lunched at the Town & Country Club, sailed at the White Bear Yacht Club, socialized at the Minnesota Club, and gathered for dinner parties at each other's homes.

One can easily imagine Cass Gilbert and his client William Lightner in 1893, walking to lunch from their offices in downtown St. Paul as they discussed the plans for Lightner's new home at 318 Summit Avenue. One of the city's top attorneys, Lightner was a partner in the firm of Young and Lightner and a vice president of St. Paul Land and Mortgage. His wife, Carrie Drake, was the daughter of E. F. Drake, builder of the first railroad in Minnesota, a state senator, and an early developer of St. Paul's Lowertown.

OPPOSITE: *The Lightner house has been called "the finest residential design of Cass Gilbert's illustrious career."* ABOVE: *Architect Tom Blanck designed the gracious, three-season porch overlooking the river valley.*

William Lightner's friends included Lucius Ordway, co-owner of Crane and Ordway, a plumbing supply firm, financier, and early investor in Minnesota Mining and Manufacturing (3M).

Before moving into their new home in 1894, the Lightners and their sons, Milton and Drake, lived in a Cass Gilbert-designed duplex at 322–324 Summit, adjacent to their new lot. The Lightners lived in the east half of the house, and Judge George B. Young, William's bachelor colleague, occupied the west half.

The Lightners' home, which historian Paul Clifford Larson calls "the finest residential design of Cass Gilbert's illustrious career," reflects Gilbert's education in the Beaux-Arts tradition and his fascination with H. H. Richardson's Romanesque Revival homes. Built at a cost of $26,988, the 8,600-square-foot mansion features a façade of brownstone mined in Bayfield, Wisconsin, and quartzite from South Dakota as well as nine graceful steps leading to the arched entry. Beyond the polished oak front door, the interior includes a grand staircase,

PREVIOUS PAGES: *ASID MN designers Marlene Hernick, Mary Ellen Gardiner, and Barbara Hafften added a period-style chandelier to complement Gilbert's original sconces and the grand staircase in the foyer.* OPPOSITE: *Gilbert's mahogany woodwork graces a corner of the living room, accentuating the arched motif found in the Richardsonian Romanesque style of the house.*

leaded windows, ornate oak and mahogany woodwork, two shower baths (a novelty at the time), a spacious kitchen, and sliding doors between the central hall, library, living room, and dining room—perfect for dinner parties and other gatherings.

William died in 1936, and Carrie continued living in their home until she died in 1944. For nearly 60 years, the Lightner residence served as an apartment building, a music studio, a guesthouse, and headquarters for a catering business. In 2006, Dick Nicholson, great-grandson of Lucius Ordway, and his wife, Nancy, bought the house. The Nicholsons have restored several architecturally significant homes in the Historic Hill District, including the 25,000-square-foot Louis and Maud Hill house on Summit Avenue.

Dick met Tom Blanck—architect, founding member of the Cass Gilbert Society, and neighbor—at one of Blanck's garage sales, and the men became good friends. Dick invited Blanck to help restore the Lightner house and return it to a single-family home. "What Dick does is a very special form of boosterism," says Blanck. "With the Lightner residence, he saw an opportunity to make St. Paul a more interesting and vibrant place."

Blanck's plans included replacing rotted beams and ceilings, eliminating eight kitchenettes, and removing the original kitchen from the basement. The architect consolidated the servery and the billiards room to create room for a new kitchen on the first floor and transformed the third-floor servants' quarters into guest rooms and an entertainment room. Inspired by Gilbert's original plans for the home, he carefully re-engineered the site to make room for a pair of detached pavilions with garages and landscaped the property. "I've worked on more than 700 projects with a couple hundred of them in the hill districts, but the Lightner house has been the largest and most delightful restoration project in my career," says Blanck.

As part of the renovation project, the Nicholsons invited the American Society of Interior Designers Minnesota Chapter and *Mpls.St.Paul* magazine to transform the house into the 2007 ASID MN Showcase Home. Using a historically appropriate palette of reds, blues, greens, and golds, the team of interior designers re-envisioned the kitchen, dining room, a music room, a gentleman's study, the 918-square-foot master suite, two bedrooms, two bathrooms, an artist's suite, a caretaker's suite, the pavilions, and a basement bierstube—a frequent feature of Gilbert's buildings, including the Minnesota State Capitol.

In 2009 John Fallin bought the home. "The Lightner house has made a beautiful home for our family," says Fallin. "We enjoy its one-of-a-kind history, the location, and the views of the river valley." Fallin has continued the home's tradition of entertaining, adding a "men's crisis center" for playing cards and smoking cigars and a dance studio below one of the garages. "Our children—Cain, Prada, and Pearl—love inviting friends over, and it never gets too crowded with all the great areas to hang out."

Just as the architects intended.

OPPOSITE, TOP LEFT: *Gilbert designed sliding doors between the dining and living rooms for easy configuration of the first floor for entertaining.* OPPOSITE, BOTTOM: *The design team of Keri Olson and Jen Ziemer updated the music room in shades of celadon with terra-cotta accents.* ABOVE: *Interior designers Shelley Bowman, Leila Lake, Cindy Abramowitz, and Pat Manning-Hanson chose bold furnishings to complement the mahogany woodwork in the dining room. Project manager John Morris of Stephenson Construction estimated in 2007 that the Lightner house woodwork would cost more than $1.5 million to reproduce today.* RIGHT: *Gilbert's magnificent sideboard has etched-glass cabinet doors.*

PREVIOUS PAGES: *For the 2007 ASID MN Showcase Home project, interior designers Randy Nelson, Nancy Woodhouse, and Jennifer Sheffert incorporated motifs from Gilbert's leaded glass into their design scheme for the living room.* OPPOSITE, TOP AND BOTTOM: *Maureen Haggerty, David Heide, and Mark Nelson designed the luxurious 918-square-foot master suite, which includes a sitting room, porch, sleeping chamber, and master bathroom.* RIGHT: *A grand staircase with carved spindles leads to the bedrooms on the second floor.* BELOW: *The master bathroom features Gilbert's original marble, leaded windows, and original toilet by Crane and Ordway. Lucius P. Ordway, a friend of William Lightner, was an early investor in Minnesota Mining and Manufacturing (3M) and the great-grandfather of Dick Nicholson.*

340 SUMMIT AVENUE   *by Dave Kenney*

Steven and Diane Anderson had few illusions that the home they purchased in 2005—the big, Italian Renaissance palace at 340 Summit Avenue—was a simple fixer-upper. They had recently restored another Summit Avenue home, a Queen Anne Victorian about six blocks away, and they knew they had a lot of work ahead of them. Whatever apprehensions they may have harbored melted away in the glow of the mansion's undeniable appeal. Every time they walked through the entry on its long side porch, they felt at home.

"It's a joyous place," Diane says. "It has a very nice spirit to it."

"We felt we had to save it," Steve adds.

The home had seen a lot of living in its 100-plus years. Commissioned in 1894 by local banker Thomas Scott and designed by architects Charles A. Reed and Allen H. Stem—the men behind such well-known edifices as the Saint Paul Hotel and Grand Central Terminal in New York City—it was one of the city's biggest residential incarnations of the popular Italian Beaux-Arts style. From the outside, its symmetrical façade, combed Indiana limestone exterior, window trim, porch columns, and decorative garland roof lining all evoked Renaissance Revival. Inside, Italianate flourishes, beginning with the black-and-white marble-tiled foyer, continued from room to room.

Thomas and Mary Clare Scott lived in the house they commissioned for only four years. George Thompson, owner and publisher of the *St. Paul Dispatch* (and later the *St. Paul Pioneer Press*) and his wife, Abigail, purchased the home in 1900. Abigail continued living there for seven years after her husband died. In 1925, businessman Samuel Shepard (of the prominent railroad construction Shepard family) and his wife, Charlotte, acquired the property and proceeded to mold it to their Continental liking. They renovated the interior with imported French, English, and Irish furnishings and fixtures, including several cascading chandeliers.

OPPOSITE: *Architects Reed and Stem turned the entry of the house sideways, as commonly seen in Italian Renaissance-style homes.* ABOVE: *Square columns decked out in filigree support the home's Beaux-Arts-style portico.*

The Shepards moved out after World War II, and in the decades following, the house lost much of its luster. New owners carved the mansion's 10,000 square feet into eight residential apartments so as to accommodate as many as 40 tenants at one time. They deferred maintenance, making repairs only when absolutely necessary. By the time Anderson purchased the house in 2005, it was in sad shape. The plumbing and electrical systems needed major upgrades. The third-floor ballroom, one of the home's most impressive spaces, had suffered serious water damage. Overgrowth almost completely obscured the backyard, with its million-dollar view of the city and the river. "It was ripped up really bad," Steven says.

Diane oversaw the redesign and renovation, and the process went on for nearly a year before the Andersons and their five children could move in. Finally, after more than half a century as a glorified boardinghouse, the mansion returned to its single-family roots.

The Andersons designed their changes to make the mansion more family friendly and homey. They transformed the elongated parlor looking out on Summit Avenue into a modern kitchen and family room. They rescued its original teak floor, nearly destroyed by water damage; the floor and the newly reproduced, pressed-tin ceiling pull the two spaces into a coherent whole. They made the second-floor sitting room into a master bedroom and reclaimed and updated the four original bedrooms on that floor for 21st century comfort.

The Andersons had one other major goal in mind when they bought and renovated their new home—to make it a showcase for music. Steven is a celebrated pianist, composer, and recording artist, and from the moment he first stepped into the house, he knew it had the makings of a superior recording studio and performance space. And now the grand foyer, with its checkerboard marble floor and live acoustics, its Bösendorfer grand piano situated at room's far end, takes on a new role as concert hall. "I'm always inspired by spaces and acoustics," Steven says. "The sound in there is just incredible. I can seat 100 people in there for concerts."

The hallway off the foyer leads to another room reconfigured for music making. It's the old library, which Steven now uses as a recording studio. Nothing like the sterile, acoustically controlled spaces in which many musicians typically record, it's a warm and woody hideaway made even more inviting by its Irish motifs and unique fireplace façade. "I sit in there, and it's just joy," Steven says. "The bluff view—it's one of those things. Even after all these years, I still look at it every day and say, 'Wow!'"

Hosting recitals and slumber parties alike, the old mansion at 340 Summit has proved its versatility. "This is a space that gets used," Steven says.

"It's meant to be shared," Diane adds. "You can't bring something like this back to life and just keep it to yourselves."

ABOVE: *The foyer's Italianate-inspired black-and-white checkerboard floor creates a mesmerizing pattern when viewed from above. The Shepard family installed a series of French-inspired chandeliers in the 1925 renovation.* LEFT: *Classical motifs festoon the fireplace anchoring the far end of the foyer-turned-performance-space.* OPPOSITE, TOP AND BOTTOM: *Wedgwood blue predominates in the dining room, located just off the foyer. Victorian scallopine fireplaces were common in the 1890s. This one was reinvented by the homeowners.*

OPPOSITE: *A stone fireplace crowned by extravagant woodwork adds classically inspired heft to owner Steven Anderson's unlikely recording studio, installed during the Shepards' renovation in 1925.* ABOVE: *The original leaded-glass door separates the main entry from the grand foyer.* RIGHT: *European hand-painted doors lead to the dining room on one side and the kitchen on the other.*

by Dave Kenney

Many people who purchase homes on Summit Avenue do so at least in part because they enjoy the challenge. To them, the prospect of restoring a warped and waterlogged hardwood floor to its original glory is invigorating rather than daunting. They get a thrill out of bringing back to life a house that once seemed on the brink of death. Larry and Pat Frattallone are not that type of people.

The Frattallones would never have considered purchasing their elegant home at 285 Summit Avenue had the house not been in excellent condition when they first encountered it in 2001. At the time, they were living comfortably in a fine home in the upscale community of North Oaks, north of St. Paul, and were in no rush leave. But Pat—and to a lesser extent, Larry—had been thinking that it might be nice to live somewhere more exciting than North Oaks. Summit Avenue was just the kind of lively urban neighborhood they had in mind, but the houses on Summit were old, and they had no desire to take on a major renovation project. That's why they jumped at the chance to buy the house at 285 Summit. "It was in perfect shape," Larry says.

The house and the property on which it sat had gone through plenty of ups and downs over the previous century. Former Congressman and U.S. Senator Henry Rice had built a two-story frame house on the site in 1882. That house survived only until 1899, when a new owner, investment banker Frederick A. Fogg, replaced it with another, more stately residence. Designed by celebrated local architect Allen H. Stem, whose previous residential works included the Italian Beaux-Arts mansion at 340 Summit, the new house was a Neoclassical gem with borrowings from the Renaissance and early American periods. Its defining exterior design elements included a columned porch, symmetrical front façade, and transoms crowning the windows on the first two levels. Topping it all off was a trio of half-moon windows fronting a grand, third-floor ballroom.

Like many homes on Summit Avenue, the Fogg house fell on hard architectural times in the years surrounding World War II. With rental housing at a premium, the house's new owners divided it into 14 separate sleeping rooms and carved out five tiny kitchens equipped with jerry-rigged gas stoves. They installed a wrought-iron gate in the main hallway to separate themselves from their tenants. Unwilling to invest in maintaining the home's elegant exterior, they covered the original clapboard with cement-asbestos siding.

ABOVE AND OPPOSITE: *Among the original Neoclassical features of this home designed by architect Allen Stem are a columned front porch and formal entrance framed by flanking sidelights and a double-arch transom.*

For four decades, the old Fogg house steadily deteriorated, its grandeur fading to a distant memory. But then in 1987, local physician Tom Harkcom and his partner purchased the home, determined to coax it back to health.

The new owners knew they were taking on a major renovation, but they didn't realize until they started getting their hands dirty just how big a job it would be. "It was pretty scary," Harkcom says. They removed the midcentury siding, tore out partitions, repaired and cleaned woodwork, recast disintegrating plaster, and completely rewired and replumbed the guts of the house.

As they worked to resolve their new home's multiple issues, Harkcom and his partner gained an even greater appreciation of its craftsmanship. The front parlor, or music room, was a prime example of the quality they encountered. Adorned with intricate plasterwork, built-in banquettes, and a charming ceiling mural (which survived the previous decades almost fully intact), it was in Harkcom's estimation "one of the more spectacular rooms on Summit Avenue." But it also was just one piece of a much greater whole. "This was really a major, important house, made with such incredible materials," Harkcom says. "When you see that English oak in the living room, that inlaid mahogany in the dining room, and that music room, you feel like, 'Wow, there's something here that needs to be restored.' It was so satisfying to fix it up."

Harkcom and his partner sold the home during the late 1990s knowing that they were leaving it in far better shape than they had found it. The Frattallones are now benefiting from their efforts. "The house has heated floors, bathrooms that actually work, a kitchen that's functional, and three air-conditioning systems," Larry points out. "You don't have to put up with very much discomfort."

Larry and Pat's presence on Summit Avenue represents a passage of sorts, one that highlights just how much this part of the city has changed. Larry grew up in a tenement house in downtown St. Paul. As a boy, he considered Summit Avenue something akin to a foreign country. "On Sundays my grandmother brought me up to Summit Avenue and showed me where the rich people lived," he says. Now having achieved considerable success in the hardware business, he lives on the same residential street that once seemed unattainable.

"It's quite a change to live here," he says. "I didn't think that I would like it, but I love sitting out on the porch with a glass of wine. You see everybody in the world go by. They're happy. They love walking this street. It's really cool."

OPPOSITE: *The entry hall's leaded-glass windows and inlaid flooring speak to the fine craftsmanship demanded by the home's architect, Allen Stem.* ABOVE: *Decorative floral tiles, hand-carved framework, and wood-burned figures above the mantel turn the dining-room fireplace into a visual centerpiece.* RIGHT: *Neoclassical forms of Greek urns, interwoven laurel garlands, egg and dart moldings, and Ionic columns complete the detailing on the fireplace surround.*

OPPOSITE, TOP: *The living room features the classically inspired details that make this house stand out from others on Summit Avenue.* OPPOSITE, BOTTOM LEFT: *Hand-carved laurel wreaths top the scalloped corner niche.* OPPOSITE, BOTTOM RIGHT: *The fireplace incorporates elaborate corbels and mirror-flanking Corinthian columns.* ABOVE AND RIGHT: *The dining room's mahogany paneling, inlaid with laurel leaves of fruitwood and ebony, creates an atmosphere of finished formality.*

OPPOSITE: *On the ceiling of the music room, one of the most beautiful rooms on Summit Avenue, decorative bas-relief garland encircles an original oil painting of the Muses, signed "S. Grafe."* ABOVE: *Daylight filters through the ornate stained-glass windows and warms the main stairwell landing.* RIGHT: *This built-in banquette is one of a pair flanking the entrance to the dining room.*

LOUIS W. HILL HOUSE

260 SUMMIT AVENUE   *by Bette Hammel*

I n 1903, Louis W. Hill, second son of James J. Hill, and his wife, Maude (Van Cortland Taylor) received a wonderful wedding present—a stately mansion right next door to his father's. Its entire design is mainstream Clarence Johnston; what is unusual is the architect's planting of English Renaissance interiors in a Georgian Revival envelope—a 200-year leap in design. The house eclipses its original elegance on 260 Summit Avenue, thanks to its meticulous restoration by owners Nancy and Dick Nicholson.

In contrast to the hovering James J. Hill house next door, Louis's red brick residence is a lighter, more evocative structure. Classical pediment tops the tall Ionic columns of its white portico, moved from the front of the original house upon completion of a major addition in 1912. Upon entering the home, visitors admire twin stairways winding from the high-ceilinged foyer, where the Nicholsons warmly greet their guests. Despite its elegance, this is clearly a family home.

Here Louis and Maude Hill raised a family of four children. Outside the home, Louis's instinctive business sense resulted in his appointment as president of the Great Northern Railway Company by his father in 1907. And through his railroad-related travels, Louis developed a love of the mountains that led to his founding of Glacier National Park. He often hiked in Canada's Waterton Lakes Park; he designed the Prince of Wales Hotel in Waterton and nine chalets in Glacier. To this designer and romanticist, the beauties of Glacier Park—and of the city of St. Paul and his father's art collection next door—became the subject of his favorite hobby, painting. He continued it until his death in 1948.

OPPOSITE: *Often recognized by its white widow's walk, the historic residence sits on a bluff overlooking the St. Paul environs.* ABOVE: *The exterior of this stately Louis W. Hill mansion, built in 1903, is of Georgian Revival design with Ionic columns, Classical pediment, and carved entablature framed in white, against a red brick façade.*

Louis Hill retained Charles S. Frost to design a two-story addition to the front façade of his home, completed in 1912. Its design included an expansive entry hall, twin stairways, four main-floor bedrooms, a ballroom filling the entire second floor, and a swimming pool in the basement. The front façade and portico were removed, and the facade was rebuilt at the front of the 30-foot addition to include the original portico.

After Louis's death, the Hills gave the property to the Catholic Church, which housed two successive Catholic organizations there. In 1998 the nonprofit Deva House bought it with plans for a hospice. In 2001 the organization changed its plans and sold it to the Nicholsons instead.

Dick and Nancy Nicholson loved history and longed for a home on the bluff. They had already remodeled a Victorian house on Goodrich Avenue, but the massive Hill residence called to them despite its need for updating: As a great-grandson of Lucius Pond Ordway,

an early 3M investor and associate of the Hills, Dick had family connections with the house, Nancy wanted a home suitable for hosting community events, and Dick loved the wood carving of Vienna-trained William Yungbauer evident through the house.

In 2002 the couple began restoration of the house. Dick was ready to preserve it for the next hundred years. The craftspeople they hired replaced the roof and the windows, installed air-conditioning, tuck-pointed the brick, and renovated the bathrooms.

Architect Gar Hargens, owner of Close Associates, transformed the butler's pantry into a modern, working kitchen (the original was in the basement) featuring two new stainless-steel sinks and an island topped with granite, while retaining the original woodwork, nickel-plated sink, and dumbwaiter. He also helped design the patio, renovated the swimming pool, and converted part of a basement laundry into a garage.

The interior, described as English Renaissance in style, speaks of Nancy's flair for color and design. She hired several decorators to help achieve the comfort she had in mind. For the original living room/library facing the bluff, they reupholstered a plump, comfortable sofa plus four accompanying chairs in damask green. These furnishings face a massive fireplace with a hand-carved, Honduran mahogany surround. Books line the walls above newly sanded

PREVIOUS PAGES: *Carpeted twin stairways meet in the high-ceilinged foyer, leading visitors down a hallway lined with paintings to a reception area overlooking the river valley. In an unusual twist, Johnston designed the interior in English Renaissance style, in contrast to its Georgian exterior.* BELOW: *This reverse view of the twin staircases leads to the front door. The home's name—Dovehill—is painted above the transom.* OPPOSITE, LEFT: *A Chinese screen hangs on the wall of the stairway leading to the ballroom.* OPPOSITE, RIGHT: *This view from the living room, through Corinthian columns, leads to a formal space featuring the family's art collection, including a bronze sculpture.*

and sealed oak floors. A palatial hallway, extending from the front of the house to the back, features a gleaming fireplace trimmed in white marble. Altogether it is an expansive, welcoming space perfect for the display of artworks including a portrait of Nancy by local artist Syd Wicker and a bronze sculpture.

The 25,000 square-foot home fulfills Nancy's wish for entertaining en masse. The original dining room is resplendent with James J. Hill's New York dining table, seating 22. A huge fireplace, surrounded by carved Honduran mahogany accented with green marble, is the perfect backdrop for a Greek frieze depicting a battle scene. Two John LaFarge stained-glass windows from James J. Hill's early home in Lowertown enhance this formal room. To the rear of the gathering space is one of the family's favorite rooms—a solarium offering stunning views of the Mississippi River, the St. Paul skyline, and the home's sweeping terraces and patio below.

From the time they made this their home, through years of painstaking renovation, family graduations, weddings, and Nancy's struggle with cancer, the Nicholsons have opened their home to benefit St. Paul nonprofit organizations including Minnesota Public Radio, the St. Paul Public Library, the Minnesota Historical Society, United Theological Seminary, the Schubert Club, Minnesota Opera, St. Paul Chamber Orchestra, and Regions Hospital. Their grand ballroom has greeted the likes of Robert Redford and Laura Bush to fundraisers as warmly as was Queen Marie of Romania, who visited the house in 1926.

At 260 Summit Avenue, the Nicholsons have happily combined preservation, hospitality, and philanthropy to the benefit of their community for generations to come.

PREVIOUS PAGES: *Local leaders and national celebrities have dined with the Nicholsons. The opulent dining room fulfills Nancy's wish for a space to host community events. Seated at James J. Hill's massive New York dining table, guests also enjoy two John LaFarge stained-glass windows and a huge fireplace surround of carved Honduran mahogany.* ABOVE: *The semicircular breakfast room, or solarium, offers splendid views of the Mississippi River and the St. Paul skyline. The Nicholsons' favorite room features original stained-glass windows by Louis Millett, white marble-clad sills, and a green terrazzo floor.* LEFT: *Nancy keeps track of events at this antique roll-top desk in a first-floor bedroom remodeled as her office.*

RIGHT: *A frieze of a Greek battle scene is inlaid into the hand-carved mahogany fireplace surround.* BELOW: *Community organizations such as the St. Paul Chamber Orchestra, Minnesota Public Radio, and the Minnesota Historical Society have gathered in the ballroom of 260 Summit. The ornate concave ceiling gives way to octagonal skylights highlighting the grand second-floor space.* FOLLOWING PAGES: *That the historic Louis Hill mansion is now a family home is evident in its big, comfortable living room and library. Reupholstered green damask chairs and an inviting sofa face another intricately carved mahogany fireplace. The hand-plastered ceiling suggests the diligence of local craftsmen in completing this unique room.*

955 SUMMIT AVENUE   *by Melinda Nelson*

By all accounts, Carlos Nelson Boynton—real-estate titan, rancher, and horse breeder—lived a big life. In the early 1900s, Boynton swept through Minnesota, North Dakota, Montana, and Maine, smashing state transaction records as he acquired and sold vast tracts of land to settlers, farmers, and speculators. In 1913, the Carlos Boynton Land Company Ranch, on 1,200 acres just west of Truman in southern Minnesota, was considered the biggest piece of land under single ownership and management outside Montana and the Dakotas.

OPPOSITE AND ABOVE: *Johnston's design features an unusual mix of Baroque Revival and Jacobean elements including ball-and-pointed finials, impish faces carved in stone, and an open porch with timber framework.*

In 1904, Boynton and his wife, Kate, commissioned architect Clarence Johnston to design a home on Summit Avenue for the princely sum of $26,000. Johnston's design, a graceful and unusual mix of Baroque Revival and Jacobean styles, included a wealth of extraordinary detail—an open porch with timber framework, one gabled and four segmental arched dormers, ball-and-pointed finials, scrollwork with impish faces carved in stone, leaded-glass windows through the house, and hand-carved wood paneling in the stable.

As befitted a man of Boynton's stature, Johnston designed the home with seven bedrooms, a ballroom, three fireplaces, two kitchens, maids' quarters overlooking the gardens, and a butler's pantry with a radiator-heated warming cabinet. In the front hall, illuminating a grinning face carved into the Honduran mahogany staircase, is a stained-glass window bearing Boynton's family crest and the words *Il Tempo Passa*—Italian for "time flies."

For those who are having fun, it flies even faster. Shari and Roger Wilsey bought the Carlos Boynton house 14 years ago. Shari recalls their first visit as if it were yesterday: "We came to the open house, and even though there were three people living in the basement and eight people living in the carriage house, I fell in love with the house. As I was coming down the staircase, Roger asked me whether I'd seen enough. I got to the bottom of the stairs and said, 'I don't think I could ever see enough.'"

Thus began another chapter in the home's colorful history, made more vibrant by Shari's abundant joie de vivre and passion for interior design, as well as by Roger's appreciation of her talents. "I thought the house was perfect before we moved in," says Roger with a laugh. "But now there's no comparison. Shari can walk into a room or a house and instantly see a beautiful picture of what it could be. Her ability to bring out the beauty that's been lost is truly a gift."

Working closely with a team of local artisans and craftspeople, Shari began restoring the home on her signature, rapid-fire timeline. "Every inch of every room needed addressing," she says. She renovated the kitchen in a week, installing three ovens, two sinks, two dishwashers,

PREVIOUS PAGES: *A stained-glass window bears the Boynton's family crest with the words Il Tempo Passa—Italian for "time flies." The central stair hall also doubles as the music room.* OPPOSITE: *Shari Wilsey used the birds on the curtain and ottoman fabric as inspiration for the color palette in the family room. The French mermaid statue is a favorite find from a Minneapolis antique store.*

a marble-topped center island, custom glass-fronted cabinets, and elegant dentil molding to match Johnston's woodwork in the dining room. "With everything I do, I respect the original flavor of the house, so nobody can tell where the remodeling starts and finishes," she says.

Room by room, Shari has layered the house with her collections of English transferware, Italian majolica, Minnesota Impressionist art, Russian religious paintings, mermaid statuary, seashells, and other treasures, including a vintage brass-and-chrome serving cart from Charlie's Cafe Exceptionale in Minneapolis and three framed sketches by Clarence Johnston of a staircase for the Hamm's Brewery headquarters, drawn in 1936. "I love the thrill of the find," says Shari. "I've been collecting art, china, and furniture at estate sales, yard sales, and farm auctions since I was a teenager, and I had my own antique shop in Stillwater for ten years. Now that everything's at home in the house, every piece seems to be part of the journey that brought us here."

Shari also turned her laserlike focus on the carriage house, the stables, and the formal English gardens. She removed layers of paint from the paneling, dug up grass to reveal the original brick pathway in the garden, and planted serpentine rows of boxwood and drifts of roses, peonies, delphiniums, and other perennials that grow vigorously in the gardens' rich soil—provided "courtesy of Boynton's horses," she notes with a smile.

In 2004, Shari, Roger, and their seven children threw a party to celebrate the home's 100th birthday. Acting as "supreme commander-in-chief," as Roger calls her, Shari cooked enough food for an army and invited family, friends, and neighbors, including Harry McNeely Jr., whose parents were the second owners of the home, and McNeely's children and grandchildren.

Recently, the Wilseys replaced the roof with slate tiles and handmade copper roof caps and spires that gleam in the sunlight. "At one point, I thought the house was done, but then a friend of ours patted me on the arm and reminded me that Shari is never finished," says Roger with a smile. "There's always some sort of big project going on. This house is an American version of Downton Abbey, and we're the staff, " laughs Shari.

When the Wilseys are working in the front yard, passersby often comment on the abundance of colorful flowers and trailing vines in the oversized urns lining the path to the house. One memorable day, a neighbor slipped a handwritten note into the Wilseys' front door, thanking Shari for "the bold and beautiful blooms gracing your front walkway . . . they lift the spirits of anyone out and about on Summit."

Shari keeps the note on the bulletin board in her kitchen where she can see it every day. "This is a happy house," she says. "Our family has had so much abundance and so much fun living here, but knowing that we're also bringing joy to Summit Avenue—that's the payoff."

ABOVE: *A hand-painted green chest echoes the original green tile that frames the fireplace, while a grandfather clock keeps the time and a barometer measures the weather.* LEFT: *The living room features Johnston's original leaded windows and etched-glass cabinet doors on each side of the hand-carved mahogany fireplace.* OPPOSITE, TOP LEFT: *Johnston designed three different geometric patterns for the carving around the fireplace.* OPPOSITE, TOP RIGHT: *Shari's majolica collection finds a home in the built-in cabinetry flanking the fireplace.* OPPOSITE, BOTTOM: *The dining room features Johnston's ornate mahogany woodwork and an original hand-painted frieze. The Wilseys inherited the ca. 1927 conference table from Roger's grandfather, founder of Indianhead Trucking, and repurposed it as a dining-room table. The vintage brass-and-chrome serving cart is from Charlie's Cafe Exceptionale.*

OPPOSITE, TOP: *In the romantic master bedroom, the barley twists on the four-poster bed echo the carved-wood legs on a pair of Irish chairs. The wallpaper and the fabric on the chairs share a similar pattern, while the hand-painted antique chest at the foot of the bed is a distant cousin of the painted green chest in the living room.* OPPOSITE, BOTTOM: *Shari layered the master bedroom with shades of ivory, champagne, and cream. She created a romantic vignette with an elegant painted writing desk, a pair of armchairs upholstered in linen, and pairs of lamps and sparkling crystal sconces.* ABOVE: *Johnston's exquisite leaded windows with green accents and an antique chandelier cast light on a collection of American still-life paintings.* RIGHT: *Hand-carved ribbons and a mascaron adorn Johnston's Honduran mahogany newel post in the front hallway, carved by the William Yungbauer firm.*

ABOVE: *Every season, Shari fills Johnston's Jacobean-inspired timber-framed porch and the walkway with oversized urns of whimsical topiary and an abundance of flowers and greenery. One memorable day, a neighbor slipped a handwritten note into the Wilseys' front door, thanking Shari for "the bold and beautiful blooms gracing your front walkway . . . they lift the spirits of anyone out and about on Summit."* LEFT AND OPPOSITE: *Colorful flowers, shrubs, trees, and vines grow vigorously in the Wilseys' garden. Roger and Shari believe that the rich soil is a gift from Carlos Boynton's horses, who lived in grand style in the mahogany-paneled stable, now the carriage house.*

by Paul Clifford Larson

Knowing the history of this house is a tonic for a faltering faith in humanity. Built by a wealthy St. Paul businessman with a great devotion to the city, it was donated by his widow to a religious order that rendered him service during World War II. When the order moved out in 1999, new owners painstakingly returned it to its rightful place as one of the great historic residences of Summit Avenue.

Samuel W. Dittenhofer (1877–1952) was a scion of a leading merchant in St. Paul. His father, Jacob Dittenhofer, had married Bettie Elsinger, uniting the two families that founded The Golden Rule, a leading upper-midwestern, dry-goods establishment. Samuel married Madeline Lang in 1905, the same year The Golden Rule incorporated and installed him as vice president and general manager.

The house at 807 was a delayed present to the newlyweds. By the time it was ready for them, at least to move into, in 1907, they had an infant daughter; a son was born two years later. Soon they had four live-in servants as well—an English housekeeper, a Hungarian cook, and two Swedish maids.

For all the love and attention poured into the planning and furnishing of the house—and into Dittenhofer's civic leadership—the couple had an equal passion for travel abroad. On 12 occasions between 1912 and 1938 the Dittenhofers steamed to France or England, the first few times with children in tow. They did not travel lightly. A customs agent noted 19 pieces of luggage with Madeline on her last trip back to the States.

During World War II, the Dittenhofers were stranded in a hotel in Paris, as Samuel had become too infirm for the weeklong voyage home. The Christian Brothers ministered to his needs, a deed not forgotten. When Dittenhofer died in 1952, his widow returned briefly to the United States to settle affairs before settling permanently in Paris.

After an appeal from the Christian Brothers in 1966, Madeline donated the Summit Avenue house and all its furnishings to the order, precipitating the home's first stage of restoration after nearly 30 years of vacancy. Joseph Tashjian, chief of staff at Regions Hospital, and Kay Savik, senior research fellow at the University of Minnesota School of Nursing, completed the process, bringing back the glow of the original woodwork, rehabilitating the house on a room-by-room basis, and blending elegant new furnishings with the fittings and fixtures from the earliest years of Dittenhofer occupancy.

OPPOSITE: *Architect Clarence Johnston specified an intricate grapevine design for the hand-carved vergeboards.* ABOVE: *Like many of the great houses of Shakespeare's time, the Dittenhofer house has a Classical symmetric entry set amidst an informal arrangement of gables and bays, with the east gable reaching down to the first floor.*

Clarence Johnston designed the Dittenhofer house in 1906, at the peak of his career and creative powers. As state architect, he was about to become absorbed in designing buildings for both the Twin Cities campuses of the University of Minnesota. But in the window between assignment and commencement of those duties, he gave Minnesota some of its finest residences. Leading the way were Glensheen (the C. A. Congdon estate) in Duluth and the Samuel and Madeline Dittenhofer house on Summit Avenue. Both were distinctively American renditions of English Renaissance architecture.

Johnston and Cass Gilbert had hotly contested earlier commissions for the Dittenhofer and Elsinger families, with Johnston generally taking the honors. His businesslike manner and long list of grateful homeowners won him multiple clients in the Reform Jewish community in St. Paul, of which The Golden Rule founders were leading members. Mount Zion Temple, just a few blocks away from 807 Summit in 1905 (and since demolished), was Johnston's major contribution to that community.

A central theme of Johnston's design is the seemingly endless sequence of subtle variations on a common motif. Kay Savik proudly points to the home's array of leaded-glass windows, carrying a different stained-glass border in each room. Finely carved human heads, each of a different figure, pop out from the walls of the dining room. The Dittenhofers may have sorted

ABOVE: *A molded plaster ceiling and carved wall paneling add a touch of Elizabethan elegance to the dining room.* OPPOSITE, ALL: *Humorous faces, ogee arches, chandelier lamps suspended from dog heads, and a richly carved buffet are all part of the Dittenhofer house's sculptural design.*

through the figures like Renaissance patrons of the arts poring over a crowd scene in a newly commissioned painting, finding people they knew and chalking off others to the painter's imagination. Two figures appear to be caricatures of Dittenhofer's Elsinger uncles.

Johnston often called on Bohemian master furniture-maker William Yungbauer to carve the wood casework in his more elaborate house commissions. The elegant strapwork balustrade of the main stairs appears to be in his hand. Each section of the balustrade was carved from a single piece of wood, probably with a combination of hand and pneumatically driven tools. Yungbauer had the skills to render the figurative carving as well.

Starting with the Dittenhofer and Congdon commissions, which he tackled in succession, Johnston enhanced his more elaborate houses with carefully designed landscapes. From the outset, a four-foot hedge set off this house from the sidewalk and street, not a privacy screen so much as an aesthetic division between home and walkway, terminating in brick piers flanking the driveway. The Dittenhofers and their architect took pains to keep the entire front of the house visible from the street, so that its dramatic cascade of gables, dormers, and chimneys was plainly visible to passersby. The rear gardens are the creation of the current owners, making use of fragmentary original material but creating anew in a manner complementary in all respects to the architecture of the house that opens into them.

PREVIOUS PAGES: *The living room's vast stone fireplace and broad hearth recall the central heating device of Elizabethan manors.* OPPOSITE: *At the foot of the grand stair embellished by Johnston's intricately carved horizontal beams and wall piers, the Tashjians' dog, Henry, finds a quiet resting spot.* ABOVE: *A succession of gables looks out over the rear gardens and pool.* RIGHT: *The ogee arch, of Moorish origin, found its way into 19th-century Spanish Jewish architecture and eventually into the buildings of several of Clarence Johnston's clients.*

1909 | A. W. LINDEKE HOUSE

345 SUMMIT AVENUE *by Melinda Nelson*

In the late 1880s, St. Paul was one of the fastest-growing cities in the country. A brightly colored map from 1888 touts the city's many assets, including 175,000 residents, 20,000 scholars, 800 freight and 280 passenger trains "in and out daily," 96 churches, 60 schools, and 16 banks with $23 million in deposits. At the time, a city historian noted that Summit Avenue, St. Paul's premier address for newly minted young moguls, was "better fitted by nature for the handsomest residences that art can design and wealth construct than any other street in America."

OPPOSITE: *Clarence Johnston designed an imposing but light-filled Tudor Villa Revival home for A. W. Lindeke in 1909.* ABOVE: *The cherub frieze over the fireplace is original to the house.*

St. Paul's moneyed class included Albert H. Lindeke, a German immigrant who arrived in America with his parents when he was 12. In 1878, at the age of 34, he cofounded Lindeke, Warner and Schurmeier, a wholesale dry-goods firm. Seven years later, when his son Albert William, or A. W., was seven years old, Lindeke built a fashionable Queen Anne home at 295 Summit Avenue for $13,000.

A. W. attended St. Paul High School and went on to Yale College, where he joined the rowing team. After graduating in 1894, he traveled abroad before returning home to St. Paul. He received his law degree from St. Paul Law School and became a partner in his father's company. A member of the Yale Club of New York City, A. W. also belonged to the White Bear Yacht Club, the Town and Country Club, and the Lafayette Club on Lake Minnetonka. In 1909, at age 36, he commissioned the state architect, Clarence Johnston, to build a home at 345 Summit Avenue, not far from his parents' house.

Situated at the corner of Summit and Virginia Street with expansive views over the river bluff, the lot had sat empty for five years. Augustus K. Barnum, a real-estate and loan magnate, built a Tuscan Villa on the site in 1879 but moved it to Irvine Park in 1909, where it existed for 70 years until vandals caused it to burn down.

Johnston designed a three-story Tudor Villa Revival home, one of the first on Summit Avenue. Built at a cost of $25,000, the house features a first story of brick and second and third stories of stucco and beam with carved wooden ornamentation. Surrounding the house is a brick wall with wrought-iron gate, illuminated by a lantern and flanked by a pair of pineapples, the traditional symbol of hospitality, carved from sandstone.

Given the home's imposing exterior, current owners Arnold and Karen Kustritz find that first-time visitors are often surprised by the abundance of natural light inside. "Clarence Johnston's houses appear to be dark on the outside, but inside, there's light in every

room," Karen says. "His windows express the wonderful natural environment outside and invite it into the house."

The A. W. Lindeke house is the second Clarence Johnston home owned by the Kustritzes. In 1970, they lived on Maryland Street in St. Paul when they spotted an ad for a Cass Gilbert-designed home on Grand Hill in the Sunday paper. They called their realtor and made an appointment to see the house. "When Arnold opened the front door, I said, "This is the house for us," Karen remembers. After the Kustritzes bought the home, they learned that it was actually designed by Clarence Johnston, thus igniting a love affair with that architect's work and a passion for buying, restoring, and selling architecturally significant homes in St. Paul.

Whether by nature or nurture, the Kustritzes' son Matt inherited his parents' appreciation for leaded windows, plaster ceilings, marble floors, and fine woodwork. "When Matt was two years old, we gave him a toy hammer, but he insisted on a real one, so we went to Seven Corners Hardware and bought him a real hammer, which he kept in his crib," Karen says.

Nearly 30 years ago, Matt started his own home-restoration business. In 2003, when his parents were living in a home on the St. Croix River, he learned that the A. W. Lindeke house was for sale. After touring the home, he called his parents and informed them that he had found their next house. As with each Kustritz project, the house quickly proved to be a labor of love.

Matt carefully renovated each room, repairing water damage, restoring plasterwork, and removing old paint and other detritus accumulated over the century. Adjacent to the kitchen was a spacious ice room, which he transformed into a bathroom. In the kitchen, beneath layers of asbestos and indoor-outdoor carpeting, Matt found beautiful, narrow, pine floorboards, which he sanded and polished to their original sheen. Karen filled the glass-fronted cabinets with 19th-century blue-and-white Chinese porcelain and hung her daughters' collection of handmade African baskets over the kitchen sink.

Throughout the house, turn-of-the-century treasures and artifacts from around the world harmonize with 17th- and 18th-century American and English furniture, Persian rugs, and oil paintings. A charming 18th-century English portrait of a rosy-cheeked young woman, entitled *Miss Meyer*, hangs in the dining room, while in the library a collection of photos taken in the Himalayas, China, and Africa by the Kustritz daughters, Anne and Sarah, lends a note of exoticism to the peaceful room.

Karen, a longtime cantor at the Cathedral of Saint Paul, board member of the Schubert Club, and member of the Metropolitan Opera Auditions Committee, often hosts concerts in the solarium. On each side of a marble wall-fountain, a blue Buddha statue, original to the house, observes every performance. "Blue is the color of sky and sea, so blue Buddhas represent infinity and changelessness," says Karen. "Every day they remind us that we are simply the caretakers of this remarkable home."

PREVIOUS PAGES: *In the solarium, a 19th-century statue of a Buddhist priest presides over a 1690 English gateleg table, which owner Karen Kustritz calls "the secret table" as she imagines the many secrets shared around it over three centuries. "The rug in the solarium chose us," she says. "I like rugs with blues and reds—the older the better."*

BELOW: *After Matt stripped layers of asbestos and indoor-outdoor carpeting from the kitchen and polished the original pine floors, Karen filled the glass-fronted cabinets with her collection of 19th-century Chinese porcelain. She hung photos and drawings by friends and copper bowls from Egypt on the walls and sun-bleached baskets from Africa over the sink. "It must be handmade, or we don't want it," she says with a smile.*

ABOVE: *Matt Kustritz stripped gray paint from the library woodwork to reveal the original green paint. Matt's sisters, Anne and Sarah, took the photograph in the Himalayas on a yearlong trip around the world. The 1740 Queen Anne Boston wing chair is covered in silk.* OPPOSITE: *Karen arranged 19th-century Chinese porcelain plates on the fireplace in the marble-floored solarium, added several years after the house was built.*

OPPOSITE, TOP: *Johnston's leaded windows cast sunlight on a 1750–1760 George II game table and a pair of 1720 Queen Anne side chairs.* OPPOSITE, BOTTOM: *Karen often hosts concerts in the living room, where a portrait of George Washington, found at a Summit Avenue estate sale, watches over the baby grand piano.* ABOVE: *The living room is furnished with English wing chairs, a 1750 tea table, and other treasures.* RIGHT: *Johnston's original tiled foyer and compact oak staircase greet visitors upon arrival.*

by Paul Clifford Larson

Historians have tied themselves in knots trying to coax the house at 821 Summit into a stylistic pigeonhole. It has a Georgian plan, both Neoclassical and Gothic ornamentation, and broad overhangs often associated with the Prairie School. But it's really none of these. All of the stylistic elements of the Johnston house were stock-in-trade for the American Arts and Crafts movement, which exercised little concern for academic precision or period pedigree. The home's monumental volume, formal composition, and magisterial air are not what we would expect from the movement that gave us the bungalow, yet it is by and large a Craftsman design.

Charles L. Johnston (1861–1942) made his fortune buying and selling farmland in Minnesota and the Dakotas. Perhaps that provides a clue to his choice of a design with bold rectilinear lines, for they recall the thousands of four-square farmhouses dotting the prairies after the turn of the 20th century. The spreading rectangular solid of the Summit Avenue house rules its site with the quiet grandeur of a four-square overlooking surrounding wheat fields. Of course it wields a bit more authority, not only from its superior size but also from its superbly fitted stone facings and monumental portico, echoed at the rear by a porte cochere.

OPPOSITE: *Warm Mankato stone facings and inventively carved brackets, column capitals, and window quoins enliven the strictly ordered façade of the Johnston house.* ABOVE: *The architecture of the porte cochere at the rear echoes that of the Neoclassical portico in front.*

Charles began his career in 1878 as a clerk in his father's loan company. In two years he rose to cashier, and by 1882 he was the tail end of D. S. B. Johnston and Son. Daniel S. B. Johnston was a phenomenon. Said to have "a personality of remarkable force" with "exceptional intellectual power," he rose to the top of the St. Paul financial community, and his sons, Charles and Alfred, rose with him.

In 1885, Charles's father established the D. S. B. Johnston Land Mortgage Company, installed Charles first as secretary, then as vice president, and confined his operations to buying and selling farmland in Minnesota and the Dakotas. Between the Panic of 1893 and Northern Pacific Railroad's release of vast tracts of land in 1898, Johnston's firm accumulated nearly 700,000 acres. Selling it off after 1900, when the Panic of 1893 had faded to memory, set the three Johnstons up for life.

Alfred preceded Charles's move to Summit Avenue by ten years. By the time Charles and his wife, Jennie Scribner Johnston, moved to their Summit Avenue home in 1911, their daughter, Edna, had married and moved away. This left the run of a very big house to the couple, a cook, and a maid. They continued to live at 821, and Charles continued to run the land company still named for his deceased father until 1942, when Charles died.

Charles Johnston's association with the architect who created his Summit Avenue home began in the late 1880s, when the couple was in their twenties and Edna was still a toddler. In 1890 the firm of J. Walter Stevens designed a Shingle-style summer cottage for them on Lake Minnetonka. The Johnstons must have liked what they got, for 20 years later they called on Stevens again—for their Summit Avenue home. Who in the firm actually created the plans of Johnston's houses is unknown, for Stevens himself freely acknowledged his shortcomings as a designer. He more than compensated for them with a sound knowledge of construction, uncompromising ethical standards, and a knack for finding and holding draftsmen of extraordinary ability. All of his buildings are constructed to the highest standard, and most of them, like the Johnston house, are masterfully designed as well.

A walk through the house clarifies its connections to the Craftsman movement. Its massive, dark-stained oak beams, matched to piers that hug the walls and high wainscoting, instantly identify the interiors with the so-called Mission style that brought equal hints of luxury and history to the humblest homes of the post-Victorian era. Here they are simply upscaled, both in size and sculptural elaboration.

The plan of the house, with the parlor and library to one side and dining room and kitchen to the other, has had such long and varied American use that it falls outside the compass of any particular style. But the show staircase and broadening of the hall give it an early American air. The heart of the Johnston house has all the spaciousness and grandeur of Georgian Revival in full bloom. The parlor to the left departs from the weighty Craftsman décor of the other interiors and extends to the west in a faceted bay. Its ceiling is adorned with a roundel of plaster-work rather than wood beams. All of these details extend Georgian Revival themes from the hall into the parlor. In the 1910s and '20s, such touches of period elegance often reflected the entry of a feminine voice into the design process: He had his library; she, her parlor.

In furnishing the house, Matt and Lori Kustritz have followed the spirit of the design's historic sources. Matt, a passionate restorationist, has helped bring ten Summit Avenue houses back to life. Persian carpets adorn the floors of 821 just as they did for the Johnstons. Authentic Queen Anne and Georgian furnishings extend the gracious sensibility of the parlor throughout the house, adding a lighter touch to the boldness of the Mission style. The furnishings resonate with the original owners' identification with their roots in early America. Jennie Johnston was a Daughter and Charles a Son of the American Revolution, tracing his heritage to William Johnston.

The Kustritzes and their two children, Alexander and Katherine, have lived at 821 for 14 years. "There's not another home our family has loved as much as this one. Living in a historic home with your children during their critical growing years is powerful," says Lori. "Our kids have had such a secure experience here. They can revel in a powerful Minnesota thunderstorm from the third floor, knowing that for more than 100 years this stone house has stood strong, protecting the family within. We are privileged to be residents and caretakers of the house at 821 Summit Avenue."

ABOVE: *A gentle curve and a flowing grapevine carving tie beam and pilaster together.* LEFT: *An 18th-century Italian landscape hangs over a Louis XVI mahogany roll-front desk, ca. 1790. The desk from Robert J. Riesberg Antiques was previously in the collection of the J. Paul Getty Museum in California.* OPPOSITE, TOP: *Matt Kustritz commissioned a master craftsman to make plaster castings from remnants of the original living-room ceiling. The castings were cured for two months before their installation on the new ceiling.* OPPOSITE, BOTTOM LEFT: *The bonnet-top Queen Anne highboy was made in Boston between 1740 and 1790.* OPPOSITE, BOTTOM RIGHT: *The Kustritz home features furnishings including an 18th-century Italian looking glass from Riesberg.*

OPPOSITE: *In the foyer, a Hudson River Valley School painting hangs over a collection of Imari porcelain and Chinese vases.* ABOVE: *The nine-foot painting in the dining room is one of a pair from a chateau in France. Lori Kustritz loves the way the painting "takes you to some other place." The American sideboard features a bellflower inlay. The Kustritzes found a dozen century-old period chairs to match the George III dining table.* RIGHT: *The dining room features an oil painting of a clergyman, the Kustritzes' collection of English silver, and several Persian-style rugs. "All our rugs have found us," says Lori. "They find their way into our house, and they always fit."*

LEFT: *The family refers to the ca. 1950 bronze statue by Gibardie as "Fleur." Depending on the season, Fleur may be dressed in a bikini or draped in fox fur.*
BELOW: *Matt loves it when guests walk into the house and mistakenly say, "You're lucky this home was in such great shape when you bought it, so you didn't have to do a lot."*
OPPOSITE: *A seascape hangs over the original green-tiled fireplace in Matt's office, formerly Charles Johnston's library. The original chandelier is tied to a double light switch on the wall—one illuminates the ceiling, the other the desk.*

5–7 HEATHER PLACE   *by Melinda Nelson*

The Twin Cities are separated only by a river, but the division between the two is legendary. There are native Minneapolitans who proudly declare they've never set foot in St. Paul and lifelong St. Paulites who claim never to have found a reason to visit Minneapolis. For the record, Clayton Halunen and David Duddingston fall into neither camp.

For seven years, Halunen and Duddingston owned a condominium at 510 Groveland near the Walker Art Center in Minneapolis. Several times a week the couple crossed the Mississippi River to visit friends and family in St. Paul and its Highland Park neighborhood, where Duddingston grew up. The men loved being part of the tight-knit 510 Groveland community, but they missed having easy access to the outdoors. When they finally decided to buy their first house, serendipity led them on a winding path across St. Paul, up Summit Avenue, and down Heather Drive, finally ending at Heather Place, where one-half of the Goodkind brothers' double house awaited its next owner.

At 510, Halunen and Duddingston lived in close proximity to their neighbors, so they were immediately captivated by the Goodkind house, the twin house next door, and the cozy, five-home neighborhood on the hill overlooking Grand Avenue. They were charmed by the home's curvaceous, Tudor Revival design and undulating Cotswold shake roof. They loved the shared circular driveway, the fountain bubbling at the center of the courtyard, and the "passover," an early version of a skyway connecting the two homes. That architect Cass Gilbert built a home for his family across the street at 1 Heather Place was a bonus.

OPPOSITE: *The west half of the Goodkind brothers' double house was designed in 1910 for Benjamin Goodkind.* ABOVE: *A vintage postcard illustrates the rear view of the double house and its gardens.*

Architects Reed and Stem designed the double home in 1910 for Benjamin and William Goodkind. The brothers were the principals of Mannheimer Brothers, a St. Paul dry-goods emporium founded by their father and uncle. Benjamin, president, lived in the west half at 7 Heather Place, while his younger brother, William, secretary and treasurer, lived next door at No. 5.

When Benjamin died in 1919 at the age of 64, Paul N. Myers, cofounder of Waldorf Paper Products Company, and his wife, Reine Humbird Myers, bought his house. In 1948, the Myerses sold it to Thomas L. Daniels, president (later chair) of Archer Daniels Midland and former member of the U.S. Diplomatic Corps, and his wife, Frances Hancock Daniels. The couple divided time between St. Paul and their summer home on Gem Lake until 1977, when they sold the Goodkind house.

Over the next three decades, the home at 7 Heather Place slowly fell into disrepair, so that by the time Halunen and Duddingston bought it in 2004, the 10,000-square-foot house required extensive renovation and plenty of TLC. They brought in crews to reface the

OPPOSITE: *Architects Reed and Stem designed the front hallway with a magnificent staircase and four leaded slit windows.* ABOVE, LEFT AND RIGHT: *Clayton Halunen and David Duddingston commissioned interior designer John Lassila to help them furnish the 10,000-square-foot house.* FOLLOWING PAGES: *The front room with a series of three French doors leading out to the terrace is a central space for entertaining—for dinner parties, fundraisers, and other events.*

stucco exterior and replace the hand-cut cedar-shake roof, the plumbing, and the electrical systems. They installed a new furnace and central air-conditioning, stripped pink paint from the woodwork in the dining room, commissioned new windows to match the original French doors, and hired a landscape architect to recreate the original terraced gardens and a gardener to maintain them.

"This house deserves all the time and money we've put into it," says Duddingston. "It's much bigger than the two of us. It's the Goodkind house, as much a part of St. Paul as the capitol, and it will always be that. We're just the people who currently own it."

Interior designer John Lassila helped the couple furnish nine bedrooms, six bathrooms, a spacious living room, a library, dining room, kitchen, butler's pantry, breakfast room, and other spaces. Halunen and Duddingston brought only a few rugs and paintings from their condominium, preferring to find antiques and other pieces that fit the age and grandeur of the home. In the cozy library, an English oil painting of a patrician gentleman with a pinky ring hangs over the fireplace. Duddingston, who is of Scottish ancestry, refers to the portrait as "Great Uncle Duddingston," while Halunen, who grew up on the iron range, says it's the president of an iron-ore mining company. "We both have a caretaker mentality about this

house," says Halunen. "Whether we're buying a piece of art, a chandelier or a sofa, we buy it for the house, not for ourselves."

The couple is well aware of the good fortune that has allowed them to be a part of the home's history. "Whenever we return home from a weekend up north, we walk through the door, and inevitably one of us comments on how lucky we are to live here," says Duddingston.

"This is truly a great house," says Halunen. "Reed and Stem really knew how to design a home. I marvel at how much thought they put into designing the proportions of the rooms, and every last detail, from the light fixtures to the silver closet hidden behind a panel in the dining room."

Occasionally, a former owner of the home or one of their relatives will pay a visit to the house. "Except for the Goodkinds, we've met somebody from every family who's ever lived here," says Duddingston. One of the couple's most cherished possessions is a calling card from the second Mrs. Daniels. In May 2006, she was visiting from California and asked her chauffeur to take her to her former abode. On her calling card, inscribed "Mrs. Thomas Leonard Daniels," she wrote, "Delighted with your work on my old lovely home." The card was tucked inside the front door, where the owners found it when they got home from work.

In honor of her visit, the couple named one of their two cats "Mrs. Daniels." The other cat, as one might expect, is "Mr. Goodkind."

PREVIOUS PAGES: *The dining room features the original pargework ceiling by Carlos Brioschi and Adolfo Minuti, plaster sculptors who also worked on Grand Central Terminal in New York. A similar ceiling in the library was damaged by water, but the couple plans to replace it.* OPPOSITE, TOP: *The owners used an antique Chinese candle lantern as inspiration for the hand-painted frieze in the dining room.* OPPOSITE, BOTTOM: *Halunen and Duddingston commissioned a landscape architect to restore the terraced gardens to their original grandeur. In 2006 they added a swimming pool and patio.* RIGHT: *They transformed an old smoking porch into a spiral staircase that leads to the basement.* BELOW: *Behind one of the panels in the dining room is a secret silver closet, painted in its original eau de nile, "but without any silver," laughs Duddingston.*

One day back in the mid-1970s, Martha Anderson filled in for her son on his newspaper delivery route. The route included a section of Summit Avenue, near what is now the University of St. Thomas. Among the homes she delivered to that day was a tidy, Prairie Style house on the 2000 block. Martha had never noticed the house before, but once she saw it, she couldn't get it out of her mind. It seemed familiar. "I grew up in Rochester and was surrounded by Arts and Crafts homes," she explains. "It was part of my DNA."

In 1978, a "for sale" sign went up outside the house. Martha had to see it. "I remember coming over to meet the real-estate agent," she says. "I came onto the porch and looked in the window and saw all this wood. I walked into the house and said, 'I have to have this.'"

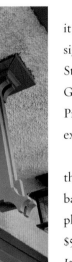

OPPOSITE:*The Beebe–Leuthold House, with its distinctive half-moon and twin-corner windows, is the only Purcell-and-Elmslie-designed home on Summit Avenue.* ABOVE: *Wooden brackets at the corner eaves incorporate an intricate V pattern, a trademark of Elmslie's ornamental motifs.*

Martha and her husband, David Anderson, didn't realize it then, but the house at 2022 Summit is one of the most signifcant Prairie Style structures in the Twin Cities, the only St. Paul house designed by Minneapolis-based architects William Gray Purcell and George Grant Elmslie. The two were masters of Prairie Style, and this home—completed in 1912—is a marvelous example of their work.

John Leuthold, a wealthy German immigrant, commissioned the home as a gift to his daughter Bess and her new husband, bacteriologist Ward Beebe. The architects based their first-floor plan for the house on Frank Lloyd Wright's "Fireproof House for $5,000," which first appeared in a 1907 edition of *Ladies' Home Journal*. The Beebe house is, in Purcell's words, "a re-transcription" of the home overlooking Minneapolis's Lake of the Isles that he and Elmslie designed for Oscar Owre, a professor of dentistry.

The Beebe house departed from typical Prairie Style design in at least one significant respect: the steeply pitched intersecting gable roof brings to mind the English Arts and Crafts movement rather than the homegrown, middle-America version of what is sometimes called "organic" architecture. Overall, though, the home is an exhibition of familiar Purcell and Elmslie design elements, including a recessed entrance, corner-set casement windows, wide eaves, and an open floor plan built around a central fireplace and raised hearth.

The Andersons did not think much about their home's backstory during their first few years as owners. "We were not very interested in the history of the house," Martha admits. "We're not decorators. We just loved the house." With four kids to rear, the Andersons could invest only so much time and money in restoring their new home's Prairie spirit. In a

ABOVE AND LEFT: *A sprawling brick fireplace and raised hearth form the hub of the home's first floor, where Elmslie-inspired stenciling binds the main living spaces into a coherent whole. The living room defines many of the Prairie Progressive tenets of design: open floor plans expanding interior views, raised-hearth fireplaces placed in the center of the room, intricate decorative stencil patterns rimming the perimeter, and the liberal use of casement windows to let in light.* OPPOSITE: *Purcell and Elmslie's belief in organic furnishings, clean lines, and color supports the homeowners' choice of Art and Crafts furniture for the space.*

first attempt at remodeling, they removed the wall-to-wall carpeting that covered the entire first level—including the kitchen—and refurbished the original wood flooring.

Not until the children were older did the Andersons think seriously about restoring their home to something approaching its original Purcell-and-Elmslie form. "We wanted to spruce things up," Martha says. "It needed painting. It needed updating. So we thought, 'Well, let's do it right. Let's see what the history of the house tells us.'" The Andersons hired Sylvestre Construction to research the house's past and draw up plans for a historically responsible remodel. The results are stunning.

Of all the changes the Andersons made during their house's renovation, none is more striking than the stenciling—reproduced from one of Elmslie's original designs—that encircles the entrance, living, and dining spaces. The line of repeating natural motifs runs between bands of dark wood, helping to create a unified space.

Other changes, while less obvious, are just as important. At some point before Martha and David bought the house, someone removed the intricately patterned glass doors that fronted the living room's built-in bookcases. Sylvestre recovered three of the doors, constructed a pair of matching side panels, and restored the cabinet to its rightful significance. The company's restoration professionals simultaneously reconstructed several light

fixtures from disassembled original pieces found tucked away on the shelves.

Many of the first-floor furnishings reinforce the house's reinvigorated Prairie character. The dining room in particular seems transported from the Progressive Era. The table, chairs, and sideboards—the renowned California architectural firm Greene and Greene designed them—are family heirlooms handed down by Martha's maternal grandfather, an early convert to the Arts and Crafts movement. The Greene and Greene pieces blend seamlessly with Purcell and Elmslie's built-in cabinets and dark-stained wood banding. In the living room, another hand-me-down from Martha's grandfather—an Arts and Crafts table lamp—forges one more link to the house's Prairie pedigree.

The result is a coherent and calm living space in which family and friends immediately feel at ease. It may lack the square footage of the mansions on Summit, but the Andersons have never needed that much room. "It's a real comfortable house," Martha says. "It's not very modern as far as openness and not hugely great for entertaining, but it's a nice house . . . It was built for a family."

OPPOSITE AND ABOVE, LEFT: *Purcell and Elmslie deviated from Louis Sullivan's established Prairie style in their design of the living room's stained-glass cabinet doors. The motif appears to be a stylized flower enclosed in a sun or full moon.*

ABOVE, RIGHT: *Arts and Crafts furniture pieces in the style of turn-of-the-century designer Gustav Stickley blend right into their surroundings.*

ABOVE: *The vintage Greene and Greene table and sideboard, handed down by Martha Anderson's grandfather, complete the dining room's Arts and Crafts ambience.* LEFT: *The dining table, made of fine-grain Honduran mahogany, features an inlaid pattern of three ebony motifs wrapped in a red oak ribbon.* OPPOSITE, TOP AND BOTTOM: *A modest vestibule, brightened by a sprinkling of blue and red tile, leads to the main-floor living area.*

by Paul Clifford Larson

Emmanuel Masqueray's name will be linked forever to the Cathedral of Saint Paul and the Basilica of Saint Mary in Minneapolis. These were his masterworks. But he was no less a master of architecture both smaller in scale and humbler in intent, and he took particular delight in rare opportunities to do residential commissions. Only three of his houses are known to survive, and two of these were for Paul and Mary Doty—a city house in St. Paul and a country house in Dellwood, near White Bear Lake. Built one after the other in 1914 and 1915, they capture the spirit of 16th-century French city and country houses in much the manner that mainstream American architecture introduced historic English themes instantly dubbed "Queen Anne."

For all the historical resonance of his work, Masqueray was determined to create buildings, in his words, "entirely of the 20th century in feeling and purpose." This was no small challenge for an architect still immersed in the imagery of his years at Paris's École des Beaux-Arts. He imparted a modern spirit to his work in giving ornamentation a bold line and confining it to key spots, in contrast to the fussy, scattered ornamentation overtaking the Queen Anne style. The curve of the staircase in the entry hall, the carved fireplace surrounds, and the simple Neoclassical moldings are elegant witness to his mastery to the pared down but visually stunning geometries at home in buildings of nearly any style. At the same time, they reflect Masqueray's effort to "embody in the composition features that gave so much charm" to buildings of earlier periods.

This was simple stuff for Masqueray. The greater challenge was to create an envelope suited to modern life. And his great triumph for the Dotys was a plan evoking a sense of privacy from the street but opening to a free-flowing space within. A deeply recessed front entry steers one along one side of the porch, maintaining the seclusion of those already sitting there. Inside, the entry hall flows into a great foyer at the center of the house, with clear views through the living room on one side and the dining room on the other, on a single, long, broad axis.

The spacious foyer must have witnessed many a large gathering. For Masqueray it likely had an aesthetic purpose as well—to give visitors room to soak up the ambience of a perfectly proportioned space and take in the grand sweep of the ground floor by rotating in place. The only significant loss of recent times is that of the columns flanking the openings to the living and dining rooms. Their purpose was not to divide but to create a ceremonial transition from one part of the space to another.

OPPOSITE: *Masqueray designed a terrace on the front elevation, connecting the living room to the outdoor space with three French doors topped by arched transoms. An arched dormer and carved-stone belt course endow the façade with an air of elegance.*

ABOVE: *A secluded passageway leads from the terrace to the entry door.*

Paul Doty (1869–1938) was a proud descendant of Edward Doty, a signer of the Mayflower Compact. Doty's career as a leading mechanical engineer had led him from management of gas and electric companies in New Jersey, Michigan, Colorado, Wisconsin, and North Dakota, to St. Paul, where he finally put down roots as vice president and general manager of St. Paul Gas Light Company in 1904. Shortly thereafter, Masqueray hired Doty's firm to design and build the gas and electrical systems in the cathedral. The architect is said to have designed Doty's home free of charge in gratitude for his work on the cathedral. One feature of the design, a central vacuuming system installed at his summer home, clearly shows Doty's expertise.

Doty was widowed in 1912, and he married Mary Reddy (1874–1947) the next year. So their house on Portland was a kind of wedding gift to themselves, a way to start fresh. While the house was still under construction, the Dotys had their first and only child, Dianna. For all the grand sweep of the ground-floor spaces, the family must have lived simply. The 1920 census shows only a single servant in the household. That year the family took a trip through France, Belgium, and Holland to celebrate, according to Mary's passport application, "Father's tercentenary."

The current owners, Larry and Mary Haeg, regard themselves as stewards of the Doty House, taking as much pride in its distinguished chain of ownership as they do in the house itself. As Larry puts it, "427 Portland is more than just a historic home. The people who passed through here made history, too—the history of a great architect, of a business and civic leader who helped build the city and the cathedral, of an airline president [Croil Hunter] . . . of a woman [Carol Anderson] who built the finest collection of antique American toys, and of the most popular performer [Garrison Keillor] in the history of American public radio."

Each of 427's owners has found the majesty of the design no obstacle to a feeling of easy domesticity. Masqueray would be pleased.

ABOVE: *The living room exemplifies Masqueray's love of bold detailing, such as modillions rather than dentils in the ceiling cove and fireplace piers that stretch to the ceiling.* LEFT: *Chairs and a lowboy rest against a wall of the foyer that gently curves to the left window bay.* OPPOSITE, TOP: *Sconces frame the Haegs' art collection in perfect symmetry opposite the fireplace wall.* OPPOSITE, BOTTOM: *The beauty and scale of the three-level spiral structure of the main staircase create a stunning view for one descending it.* FOLLOWING PAGES: *Like many of Masqueray's domestic interiors, the dining room has unexpected recesses and projections, all perfectly scaled and proportioned. The soothing celadon color of the walls was inherited from previous owners.*

O Lord we thank Thee
for this food
For every blessing,every good
For earthly sustenance and love
Bestowed on us from heav'n above.
Be present at our table Lord.
Be here and everywhere adored
Thy children bless and grant that we
May feast in paradise with thee.

OPPOSITE, TOP: *At the entry side of the foyer, staircases up and down curve gently against each other and link the space to the dining room.* OPPOSITE, BOTTOM LEFT: *A classically designed, built-in arched hutch in the dining room reaches toward the 13-foot-high ceiling.* OPPOSITE, BOTTOM RIGHT: *A canted fireplace adds an air of gentility to the dining room. The prayer on the overmantle was inscribed by the previous owners.* ABOVE: *The kitchen features original cabinets, a steel table, maple flooring, and an inherited pot rack.* RIGHT: *Masqueray might himself have been proud of the expanded kitchen—for its openness, simple lines, and abundant light.*

by Dave Kenney

Few homes on Summit Avenue pique the public's curiosity as thoroughly as the wood-clad Colonial Revival tucked behind a wrought-iron fence just a few doors up the street from the James J. Hill House. It's not so much the home itself as the people who have lived in it. For many years the residence was that of one of St. Paul's wealthiest and most prominent families—the Weyerhaeusers. More recently it has become associated with another well-known public figure. More on that in a moment.

The house at 294 Summit Avenue is the second to sit on this lot. The first one, built in 1858, belonged originally to Henry Neill Paul and can be seen along with the Stuart house at 312 Summit in Joel Whitney's famous dog-sled photo. The Paul house was demolished during the 1890s, and the lot sat vacant for about 20 years.

In 1919 George Lindsay, a business associate of lumber baron Frederick Weyerhaeuser, commissioned a new house for the site. Designed by the Boston architectural firm of Parker, Thomas and Rice, the home featured typical Colonial Revival accoutrements including a symmetrical façade, wood siding, shuttered windows, dormers, and a formal, column-flanked front entrance. Among the more unexpected additions were a charming, open-air "tea house" on the back terrace and a separate structure—complete with indoor swimming pool—on the lower-bluff portion of the property. (The pool house now belongs to the owner of a separate property just down the hill.)

In the early 1930s, Weyerhaeuser's grandson Frederick King (F. K.) Weyerhaeuser and his wife, Vivian O'Gara Weyerhaeuser, acquired the home. F. K. was familiar with the neighborhood since his grandfather—and later his uncle, Rudolph—lived at 266 Summit. In 1941 the Weyerhaeusers hired local architect William Ingemann to oversee a major addition to the house's east end. Ingemann's design included a new pantry, study, and dining room on the main floor and a new master-bedroom suite on the upper level. A boiler explosion in the summer of 1942 ignited a fire that threatened to destroy the entire house, but firefighters managed to control the blaze before it did too much damage.

The Weyerhaeuser family lived at 294 Summit for nearly half a century, and over the years their house became something of a symbol of St. Paul wealth and privilege. (Who but a Weyerhaeuser could afford to place a live bison in his front yard just to poke fun at visitors

LEFT: *Symmetry, so clearly on display at 294 Summit, was a hallmark of Colonial Revival style. The wrought-iron fence apparently dates to the home's Weyerhaeuser years.* ABOVE: *The back porch affords a view of the Mississippi River Valley and the High Bridge.*

who considered St. Paul an unsophisticated cow town?) Long after the last of the family moved away, people refer to the home as the "Weyerhaeuser house."

Today the house that George Lindsay built and the Weyerhaeusers expanded is home to the family of another prominent Minnesotan—author, humorist, and radio personality Garrison Keillor of *Prairie Home Companion* fame. Keillor and his wife, Jenny Nilsson, purchased the house in 2008. They love how the interior spaces, especially the living room, feel roomier and more open than those in their previous home, on Portland Avenue. "This house is much more open in every way," Nilsson says. "The rooms are expansive. And the light—there's lots and lots of light."

The living room, which beckons from just beyond the foyer, is an unusually broad space, affording stunning views of the Mississippi River valley. It creates the impression of two rooms in one: a comfortable seating area set in front of an original fireplace on one end and a floor-level stage featuring a grand piano on the other. It's a frequent setting for fundraisers and informal, after-show gatherings. "It's really ideal for that," Nilsson says. "This house can hold a lot of people."

Despite its made-for-entertaining attributes, the house maintains a remarkably lived-in atmosphere. Keillor and Nilsson bought almost no new furnishings when they moved to 294. They just transplanted everything from their previous home. Their interior designer, Tom Gunkelman, was under strict orders to make everything, including the living room, as inviting as possible. "I told him I didn't want one of those living rooms that's so beautiful that 'God forbid somebody should spill,'" Nilsson says. "Every part of a house should be comfortable and relaxed."

That preference for simplicity and informality permeates the house. The artwork on display tends toward traditional landscape and seascape motifs. The words of a familiar table blessing form the focal point of the dining room, just as they did in the family's previous home. As in many modern homes, the kitchen is the fulcrum of family life and, in this case, of work life, too. "Garrison can work anywhere," Nilsson says. "Theoretically he's going to work in his office, and sometimes he'll go in there, but he gravitates to the kitchen or dining room on his laptop. And everyone else just goes where he does."

Keillor and Nilsson have found in the old "Weyerhaeuser house" a perfect home for their lifestyle. "The nice thing about this house is you can be home all by yourself and feel very comfortable," Nilsson says. "Or you can be comfortable with 50 people in the house. It works either way."

ABOVE AND OPPOSITE, TOP: *The rug underneath the piano features churches, townscapes, and other motifs that call to mind Keillor's fictional Lake Wobegon.* LEFT: *A contemporary snowscape by Maine artist Ralf Feyl receives prominent display in the living room's music wing.* OPPOSITE, BOTTOM: *The living room appealed to Nilsson and Keillor because it was large enough to accommodate the furnishings that interior designer Tom Gunkelman chose for their former home.* FOLLOWING PAGES: *Books line the walls of the cozy, first-floor library.*

ABOVE: *A stairway leads to the second floor from the central foyer.* LEFT: *The living room's French doors open onto a charming stone courtyard.* OPPOSITE, TOP: *The words of an 18th-century table blessing overlook the dining room, with its stunning views of the river valley.* OPPOSITE, BOTTOM LEFT: *A book-lined hallway leads to the dining room and, beyond that, Keillor's office. Keillor and Nilsson added several new bookcases to accommodate their book collection.* OPPOSITE, BOTTOM RIGHT: *An example of what could be called Prairie Home Companion décor marks the path between the kitchen and the living room.*

977 SUMMIT AVENUE   *by Bette Hammel*

The Roaring Twenties were in full swing when Louis Silverstein, president of a women's wear wholesale company, and his wife, Rose, built a Colonial Revival/Mediterranean Revival residence at the corner of Summit Avenue and Chatsworth.

Minnesota architect Peter J. Linhoff planned this duplex for the Silversteins and Rose's Russian mother as the last and largest of the 18 houses he designed over 17 years on Summit Avenue. The home's hipped green-tile roof, vertical arched casement windows with balconies, and street-facing terrace with wrought-iron railing lent further prestige to the avenue. Over the decades, however, the trees and shrubs shading the house grew so profusely that their greenery blocked the light from the interior.

Enter the 21st century and two prospective homeowners—Karen and David Olson—looking for an attractive urban site with nearby amenities. Though they lived in a newer home in North Oaks and knew from earlier experience what renovation might involve, they were willing to take on an older home in the right location. At first glance, they said no to the Silverstein house. "Too dark, too much deterioration," said Karen. But they loved the property and the structure's basic character, and they realized its possibilities.

In 2008, they "took the plunge" and called on the David Heide Design Studio, known for its restoration of historic properties, to undertake the renovation. The Olsons wanted to convert the duplex into two separate condo units so that their daughter, Amy Olson, and her husband, Daniel Sigg, could live upstairs. Both families had been considering such an arrangement for their next stage of life.

After a thorough study of the home, including its leaky roof and rotted interior walls, Heide decided a complete renovation—of both interior and exterior, thus requiring adherence to the guidelines of the St. Paul Heritage Preservation Commission (HPC)—was in order. Heide and his contractors transformed the stately old home from top to bottom while retaining its historic character and converting it to two condos for modern living. The project took two years and involved a team of experts in historic renovation. In 2011, both families moved in.

The replacement of windows and doors provides a prime example of this remarkable restoration effort. The original windows and terrace doors had been removed from the front façade and replaced with smaller, modern casement windows and smaller, standard-sized doors. With the exterior stucco removed, the architects were able to determine the size and framing of the originals. HPC guidelines allowed the installation of all new windows in the original size and configuration. Now the Olsons, who live on the first floor, say the biggest change is "the way natural light just pours in."

OPPOSITE: *David Heide Design Studio transformed this 1924 Spanish Colonial Revival residence into two modern condominiums for two generations. Architect Peter J. Lindhoff initially created it as a duplex featuring a hipped green-tile roof for merchant Louis Silverstein. Today the roof wears new green tiles, and the terrace balustrades and stucco façade have been replaced.* ABOVE: *Forms were used to cast the Mediterranean over-door ornament into the new plaster replicas.*

ABOVE: *The designers retained the handsome living room with its original fireplace and dining area in the bay. Adhering to HPC guidelines, they installed new windows throughout the home in their original size and configuration.* LEFT: *A traditional white console links the entryway to the living room.* OPPOSITE, TOP: *Upstairs and downstairs living rooms share identical footprints, one using modern design and the other, traditional motifs.* OPPOSITE, BOTTOM: *A Saarinen womb chair and other Modernist furnishings give the owners' daughter's family home upstairs a more contemporary look.*

The totally refreshed exterior is now clad in new stucco and a new, green-tile roof. The firm that made the original clay tiles—the Ludowici Company, very much alive today—manufactured the new ones as well. Some of the original tiles now grace the new, four-car garage in back. On the terrace, the long-missing balustrade has been recreated in new cast stone, and newly duplicated plaster lunettes decorate the tops of the arched windows.

On the main floor, Heide retained the Classical archways in the hallways and used arches in other rooms. The still-handsome living room retains its original fireplace surround and the pleasant dining area facing the bay windows. Adjoining this room through curved glass doors is a sunny, modern kitchen, finished in white with touches of the period such as a round, wood breakfast table.

To ensure that the renovation would function well for this modern working family, the architects rearranged some rooms. For example, the old kitchen became a comfortable new family room for the Olsons, and two bedrooms across the hall became one master suite with sizable bath. "Our bath is a work of art," says Karen, citing St. Paul cabinetmaker John Frost, who crafted a circular cabinet of rose-colored marble topped with a mirror.

Toward the rear of the Olsons' unit, the architect placed a small addition to serve as a separate entrance for the family upstairs and provide a sizeable rooftop terrace for outdoor

BELOW: *For improved function, the designers switched some rooms. The first-floor kitchen, now appointed with white cabinets and a round wood table, was once the family room.*
OPPOSITE: *The younger family upstairs wanted an ultramodern kitchen. Stainless-steel countertops on an oval island, rust-colored glass tiles, and modern cabinetry fill the bill. Their new abode also includes office space, music room, and guest rooms.*

enjoyment. Another, much smaller addition houses office space for Karen and David, as well as a new back-door entrance.

The basement provided an interesting historical feature for renovation. Tuck-in garages were the first common way of accommodating the automobile within a house plan, and in 1924, a two-car garage took up part of the basement. Says Heide, "We took advantage of that space—and created two guestrooms with outdoor courtyard where the driveway used to be." The team converted the rest of the basement into a TV-family room and catering kitchen.

For the condo unit upstairs, the design team created what Amy and Daniel wanted—a contemporary living space, complete with ultra-sleek kitchen, the latest in appliances, office space, and music room. The family enjoys the same natural lighting and sustainable features evident through the house.

Given the extensive property (105 feet on Summit and 280 feet back), the designers were able to grant their client's wish for a swimming pool, tennis court, side patio and garden, and four-stall garage—features seldom found in homes along this Victorian boulevard.

All the members of this family of tennis players, walkers, students, workers, doctors, and musicians say they love living on Summit Avenue, near its churches, colleges, and other historic homes and not far from the Grand Avenue shops. They love being part of the history of this 150-year-old property, whose front door displays a plaque with these words:

Historic Hill District
Built in 1924
National Register of Historic Places

OPPOSITE: *A traditional, round dining table creates a gracious scene in the bay at one end of the living room. An arched doorway leads to the kitchen.* ABOVE, LEFT: *Next to the master-bedroom suite is a bathroom outfitted with a stunning circular cabinet. St. Paul cabinetmaker John Frost crafted the new piece of rose-colored marble and topped it with a mirror.* ABOVE, RIGHT: *In preserving the historic character of the house, Heide used existing archways in the hallway and added a few more in other spaces.* RIGHT: *In their top-to-bottom renovation, the design team created a major back landscape transformation. They built a new garage and provided for office space, swimming pool, tennis court, and space to garden on the grounds.*

B y the 1920s, the replacement of smaller and hopelessly out-of-date homes on Summit Avenue was commonplace. Egil and Rachel Boeckmann upped the ante. The home on the lot they acquired was one of the great houses of the avenue. Designed by an eminent Chicago architect and with a carriage house by Cass Gilbert, the Daniel Noyes estate carried all the majesty of the Gilded Age of the 1880s and '90s. But even high Victorian fashion had become passé, and it was time for replacement. Like many of their contemporaries, the Boeckmanns wanted a design resonating specifically and unmistakably with America's colonial past.

To assure that their new home carried the proper pedigree, the Boeckmanns called on outside talent. Many years earlier James J. Hill had brought in Boston's Peabody and Stearns—and building stone from Connecticut—for a Romanesque design worthy of the great H. H. Richardson. Now Hill's daughter Rachel hired renowned society architect David Adler to plan a Colonial Revival that could pass muster anywhere back east. Adler's reputation not withstanding, as a true daughter of James J. Hill, Rachel Boeckmann (1881–1967) made it clear that every architectural decision, minor or major, must pass by her. The master bedroom must be reshaped, the flowerboxes redesigned. Her participation was costly: Adler produced 164 detail drawings along with 838 supporting documents, many of them exchanges between architect and client. After they spent a couple of years working out the plan and its details, construction began, in 1928, with completion in 1930.

OPPOSITE: *In the 1920s, Colonial Revival houses sprang up in nearly every city and suburb in America, but the Boeckmann house stands out for the refinement of its proportions and detailing. The architect took special pains to produce the effect of quoined corners by grouping the brick to imitate stone blocks.* ABOVE: *Colonial entries commonly had overhead "lights" (a window or bank of windows) to illuminate the entry. Interrupting the segmental arch above the door was purely ornamental.*

Loosely based on Cliveden (the Benjamin Chew House) in Germantown, Pennsylvania, the Boeckmann home's proportions closely adhered to the Golden Ratio (approximately 8x wide by 5x high) beloved by ancients and revered by academics. The brickwork in the corners projects into quoins, a divided transom and broken arch surmount the entry, the attic huddles within the lower slope of a gambrel roof, and the roof proliferates with chimneys (ten)—all hallmarks of a mid-18th-century Georgian manor. What was not Georgian was the cost—$120,000.

Though lacking the professional credentials of his peers, Adler had gained wide respect for his sensitive adaptations of classical styles to fashionable townhouses and opulent country

PREVIOUS PAGES: *The Boeckmanns'*
stair hall was spacious enough to accommodate
sitting-room furniture. Departing guests
enjoyed an exit with as many architectural
trappings as the entry. OPPOSITE:
The classic simplicity of Adler's fireplace
surround contrasts with the elaborate
carving above the mantel. Garlands, drapes,
and a strangely proportioned eagle all have
Colonial precedents.

houses. His work ranged geographically from Chicago and the Midwest to the wealthy suburbs of cities on both coasts. He followed a principled aesthetic: classically ordered façade and plan, evocation of grand themes from history, elegant employment of materials, and restraint in detail.

The challenge for Adler (and his sometime partner in business, Robert Work) was to transform a reverential echo of colonial history into an original and modern statement. As in all Georgian houses of manorial stature, the stair hall just inside the entry was the most prominent room in the house. Adler made it as spacious as possible by placing the base of the stairs at the rear of the hall, with most of the staircase running along the side. This opened up the plan, inviting a clear view through the vestibule, the stair hall, and the living room, into the rear gardens beyond. Accustomed to working on much grander sites, he made up for it by designing gardens with a magnificent interplay of flagstone and geometrically trimmed and arranged plantings. Such adventurous touches earned grudging admiration from the more progressive architects of his day.

Like all Hill's children, Rachel married a person of sound social birth on an upward trajectory. Egil Boeckmann (1881—1955) first achieved local renown in football, when he scored the final touchdown in the legendary Minnesota–Michigan game of 1903 that gave birth to the Little Brown Jug. Like Rachel's father, he also had a farm north of St. Paul, where he bred and raised cattle. The Boeckmann summer estate, also designed by Adler, embraced 200 acres and a lake in Dellwood near White Bear Lake. Between the building of his summer estate and his St. Paul home, Boeckmann repeatedly won prizes at the Minnesota State Fair for his Holsteins.

Boeckmann's lasting accomplishment was professional. As an eminent, general-practice physician with a specialty in ophthalmology, he was a founding member of the Minnesota Society for the Prevention of Blindness. His connection to the Hills also gave him entry to the famed Jekyll Island Club south of Savannah, Georgia, where he could rub shoulders with the Morgans, Rockefellers, and Vanderbilts.

The Boeckmann house has enjoyed a history of fine stewardship. Its construction supervisor and foreman were both from Adler's office. The Boeckmanns lived in the house with four servants and two children, Mary and Gertrude, who continued to maintain the property after their parents' death. Current owner and resident John R. Rupp has painstakingly restored interior finishes and preserved the stunning landscaping of what St. Paul historian Ernest Sandeen called "one of the best-designed houses on Summit Avenue."

ABOVE: *Abundant natural light was as important to Adler as understated decoration and pleasing proportions. The living room looks to the gardens in the day and focuses on the fireplace wall at night.* LEFT: *A Murano glass collection below a serene landscape creates a quiet moment in the living room.* OPPOSITE, TOP AND BOTTOM: *The simple Neoclassical moldings and white walls of the Boeckman interiors invite artfully placed paintings and show off the delicate profiles and natural wood tones of period furniture.* FOLLOWING PAGES: *Adler placed the dining-room fireplace on the wall facing the sideyard, making it a focal point of the room all hours of the day. The fireplace surround and overmantel are sculpted in architectural fashion, echoing the motifs of the exterior.*

OPPOSITE, ALL: *Adler combined clean, rectilinear lines and gracious curves with great dexterity. The library bay and turning of the upstairs staircase are especially elegant examples of the latter. The Rupps enjoy combining their art collection with period furniture to create elegant vignettes throughout the house.* ABOVE AND RIGHT: *Though closely adhering to the strictures of Georgian Revival style, the Boeckmann interiors show a great range of moods—from the restful, natural paneling and bold Neoclassical touches of the library to the white, processional spaces that lead the eye and feet from vestibule to living room.*

ST PAUL: WALKING

The old city of saints opens its hand again this morning,
    its claw of money and glass rosaries.
I never say no.
Together we have broken bread, promises, hearts,
    Whatever drags beneath our muddy river.
I put my bare hand on the red stone of the millionaire's house:
    It sizzled like water in a black pan.
Sometimes I think I will hold forever the hand of this city;
    it shakes its fist of beer and greenhouses at me,
    its long death sways on the stem of an orchid even in winter.

—PATRICIA HAMPL

GOVERNOR'S RESIDENCE *(above)* William Channing Whitney designed this Tudor Revival home in 1912 for St. Paul lumberman Horace Hills Irvine. His family lived at 1006 Summit Avenue until 1965, when the Irvines' two youngest daughters, Clotilde (Coco) Irvine Moles and Olivia Irvine Dodge, gave the house to the State of Minnesota for use as the governor's residence. The property is on the National Register of Historic Places and is part of the locally designated Historic Hill District.

OVERLOOK PARK (*above*) Public Art Saint Paul made sure this outstanding work of public art, a bronze eagle sculpted by Augustus and Louis Saint-Gaudens, was moved to Overlook Park at Summit Avenue and Ramsey Street in 2004. Originally known as the New York Life Eagle, it previously held court over the company's downtown building.

CATHEDRAL OF SAINT PAUL (*left*) The great granite Cathedral of Saint Paul, designed by French architect Emmanuel L. Masqueray, dominates the city skyline. Archbishop John Ireland brought Masqueray to St. Paul, where the two developed its scheme. Both men barely lived long enough to see its dedication, after more then ten years of construction, in 1915.

UNIVERSITY CLUB (*below*) No doubt F. Scott Fitzgerald hung out with friends at the University Club—at 420 Summit Avenue—designed by local architect Allen Stem in 1912. The Tudor Revival clubhouse is still a favorite of the literary crowd and others who enjoy its views of the city skyline and the Mississippi River valley below.

JAMES J. HILL HOUSE (*above*) The biggest
home in St. Paul, the Hill house sprawls over
36,000 square feet on five floors. Designed by
Boston architects Peabody, Stearns and Furber
in Richardsonian style, the red sandstone
Romanesque Revival structure eventually
was donated to the Archdiocese of St. Paul
and Minneapolis; the Minnesota Historical
Society acquired it in 1978. The house is well
worth visiting for its unique interiors.

NATHAN HALE PARK (*right*) A statue of
Revolutionary War patriot Nathan Hale by
William Ordway Partridge—commissioned
by the Daughters of the American Revolution
as a gift to the city—has stood at the corner
of Summit and Portland Avenues, with only
short departure for repair, since 1907.

COCHRAN PARK (*above and right*) The statue *Indian Hunter and His Dog* by St. Paul native Paul Manship (sculptor of *Prometheus* at Rockefeller Center, New York) stands poised above the fountain in Cochran Park at Summit and Western Avenues. This small pocket of land became a delightful little park in 1924, thanks to donors Emelie (Walsh) and Thomas Cochran.

CONVERSATION IN THE GARDEN (*left*) The owners of this garden in Crocus Hill thought so highly of 32 of their friends and family members that they hired Minneapolis sculptor Stuart Nielsen to create a piece that features carved sandstone profiles of their faces along the wall. Nielsen named the work *Conversation in the Garden (1999)*.

247

F. SCOTT FITZGERALD BIRTHPLACE (*below*) Originally known as San Mateo Flats, this standard-looking apartment building at 481 Laurel Avenue marks F. Scott Fitzgerald's birthplace (1896) and home for two years before the family's move to Buffalo, New York. After undergoing various subdivisions, the building was converted to condominiums. The architect was Frederick A. Clarke.

COMMODORE HOTEL (*above*) This apartment hotel at 70 Western Avenue, now condominiums, is best known to St. Paulites for its Art Deco barroom, widely considered a haunt of F. Scott and Zelda Fitzgerald though it was not added until the late 1930s, more than a decade after the couple left the city. Built in 1921 in a mix of styles, the massive brick building is the work of Minneapolis architect and engineer Alexander Rose. German-born set designer Werner Wittkamp created the elegant, intimate bar.

St. Paul Academy *(opposite, top)* F. Scott Fitzgerald was a student in this building at 25 North Dale Street from 1908 to 1911. Thomas Holyoke designed it in 1903 as the Academy Professional Building, but it soon became St. Paul Academy, a private school for boys. The school eventually moved to another address, but in 2006, Aaron Dysart's statue of the young Scott appeared on the front steps.

W. A. Frost *(right and below, right)* Originally known as the Dakotah Building, W. A. Frost— the restaurant at Selby and Western Avenues— derives much of its charm from its 19th-century architecture and ambience. The red brick building sports an inviting, shade-treed patio, making Frost's a popular Twin Cities retreat.

Blair House *(left)* A Victorian-style castle still exists at Selby and Western Avenues in St. Paul. Blair House, now housing condos and commercial tenants, is a festival of turrets, parapets, gables, and bays. Its four inner courts, narrow but well-lit, sit on a rugged stone base. Designed by Hermann Kretz and William Thomas in 1887 and renovated by W. W. Orfield and Associates in the 1980s, the building is a romantic complement to W. A. Frost, just across Western.

MINNESOTA STATE CAPITOL *(below)* At age 35, architect Cass Gilbert of St. Paul astounded the field when he won a design competition for the Minnesota State Capitol in 1895. Today the glistening white marble structure with its magnificent dome and golden horses, as beautiful inside as it is outside, is still the pride of Minnesota. Miller Dunwiddie Architecture initiated a phased restoration in 1983, and now, 108 years after its completion in 1905, the capitol is under massive restoration by HGA Architects and Engineers.

MADAM NINA CLIFFORD *(left)* The lovely wooden lady presiding over the front yard of 435 Summit Avenue is none other than Nina Clifford, owner of one of St. Paul's early brothels, formerly located below the foot of Summit Hill. The statue, chain-sawed from burr oak, suggests her peering down the street in search of customers.

MOUNT ZION TEMPLE *(opposite, bottom)* Local architects consider St. Paul's oldest remaining Jewish synagogue—at 1300 Summit—a brilliant work of Modernist architecture. Its architect, Eric Mendelsohn, had fled to the United States from Nazi Germany in 1941. Dedicated in December 1954, the temple was renovated in 1996 by Bentz, Thompson and Rietow. In 2004 Mount Zion merited a Heritage Preservation Award from the SPHPC and the St. Paul AIA for "respectful ways of bringing a Modernist landmark into the 21st century."

ESTABLISHED AS ST. LUKE'S CATHOLIC CHURCH,
RENAMED ST. THOMAS MORE CATHOLIC CHURCH
(*left and detail*) This venerable church, renamed after St. Luke's
2008 merger with another parish, graces Summit Avenue with
a masterful Indiana limestone monument in the French and
Italian tradition of European churches. It is notable for its rose
window and sculpture of the humanitarian St. Thomas More.
John T. Comes of Pittsburgh was its architect; upon his death
in 1922, others took over to complete construction in 1925.

VIRGINIA STREET CHURCH (*above*) Founded as the
Swedenborgian Church in 1887, this small church tucked away
on Virginia Street is a playful example of Cass Gilbert's early
penchant for variety in style and size. The clapboard-clad church
stands out for its octagonal bell tower, narrow spire, shingled
roof, and river-boulder base. Clarence Johnston designed an
education wing for the building in 1922.

MACALESTER'S OLD MAIN *(above)* Old Main, designed by Willcox and Johnston and built in 1887, is the oldest remaining building at Macalester College. Almost every Macalester student has had classes in this massive Romanesque-style red brick building, broadly recognized by its sharply pointed gables. Shepley Bullfinch of Boston renovated Old Main in 1993.

GERMANIC-AMERICAN INSTITUTE *(left)* The George W. Gardner house, a Georgian Revival structure of Kasota stone, was designed by Thomas Holyoke in 1905. The house has been in institutional hands since 1948 when the sisters of the Order of St. Benedict owned it. In 1965 the home became headquarters for the Volkfest Association, renamed the Germanic-American Institute.

WILLIAM MITCHELL COLLEGE OF LAW *(opposite, top left)* The college opened in 1976 at 875 Summit Avenue, in the former Our Lady of Peace High School. Originally St. Luke's School, it was designed by Ellerbe and Company in 1931. The historic building remains the centerpiece of the campus, expanded in the 1990s by Winsor/Faricy Architects and in 2005 by Perkins+Will.

CHAPEL OF ST. THOMAS AQUINAS (*above*) One of the oldest, most notable buildings on the University of St. Thomas campus is the Chapel of St. Thomas Aquinas on the north side of Summit. Completed in 1918, the Renaissance Revival worship space was designed by Emmanuel Masqueray, architect of the Cathedral of Saint Paul.

BUTLER HOUSE (*left, middle*) This lovely lemon-colored house at 516 Summit, built in 1914 for William Butler, one of five brother builders, is primarily notable for its occupant Sinclair Lewis, who lived there in 1917–18. Lewis dubbed it Lemon Meringue for its brick façade and the rough stone surfaces that "looked like whipped cream." The Beaux-Arts-inspired structure with green-tile roof adds color to the avenue.

HOUSE OF HOPE PRESBYTERIAN CHURCH (*left*) Built in 1914, the House of Hope complex adds a quietly impressive English Gothic presence along Summit Avenue. The complex includes a church with bell tower, stained-glass windows, library, chapel, and education wing. The architects were Cram, Goodhue, and Ferguson of Boston. Ralph Adams Cram was the acknowledged master of Gothic Revival in the United States. The sanctuary is a favorite performance space of the St. Paul Chamber Orchestra, thanks to the acoustics afforded by its timber-beamed ceiling. Its floor tiles are by Pewabic Pottery of Detroit.

ACKNOWLEDGMENTS

by Karen Melvin

Some people say that St. Paul is the last city of the East and Minneapolis is the first of the West. The reputations of Summit Avenue and the Historic Hill District—from the early years of Minnesota's statehood through the exuberant Victorian aesthetic and beyond—made them a logical choice for my next book about the architecture of the Twin Cities.

Last summer, walking along with my camera to shoot the details of the boulevard's grand façades, I saw the history of St. Paul's architecture unfolding. I was impressed by the sheer volume of interesting shapes and forms of ornamentation on the houses I passed. There were volutes, caryatids, turrets, colonnades, gargoyles, cartouches, cupolas, quoins, Ionic columns, Greek friezes, and many others—their colors and shapes rooted in East Coast sensibilities. That first, short visual journey was enough for me to want to know more about the story of Minnesota's grandest boulevard.

Many people opened doors and pointed me in the right direction. Lifelong resident of the neighborhood and talented designer Shari Taylor Wilsey introduced me to many other residents who have carefully restored and preserved their homes. She provided much-appreciated support through styling and propping of the interior scenes. Sarah Kinney, Tom Blanck, Jim Sazevich, Aaron Rubenstein, Tomas Hardy, and Larry Millett, whose AIA guide to Summit Avenue proved invaluable, provided information as well.

A crew of assistants and interns from local photography schools helped me through the long hours and intense days of shooting. They include Micah Helling-Christy, Antonio Rodriquez, Won-Sik Kim, Clark Quinn, Rachel Henn, Sue Tschida, and Ann Schley. Set designer Jay Bruns also styled several of the homes.

A gifted cast of writers wrote compelling stories about the original homeowners, structures, architects and those who followed: Architectural historian Paul Clifford Larson also generously edited writer's manuscripts for historical accuracy, opened files, and provided archival photography. Bette Hammel, "a St. Paul girl," inspired me with her diligent research and lively writing style. Melinda Nelson brought vibrancy and grace to the interior-design stories. Dave Kenney, a two-time Minnesota Book Award winner and engaging storyteller, rounded out the mix.

Thanks to my husband, architectural photographer Philip Prowse, for his wonderful work in photographing several of the exteriors. His unwavering support, guidance and advice carried me through the process of producing the book.

The hardest-working man in radio, Garrison Keillor contributed the foreword, for which I am very grateful, and Patricia Hampl gave the use of her poem "St. Paul: Walking."

Many thanks to editor Ellen Green, who kept the manuscripts flowing and strove to ensure historical and grammatical accuracy, and to Ellen Huber, a book designer of exquisite taste, who compiled all our words, photos, and illustrations in this beautiful volume. Narda Lebo, a lifelong friend and gifted illustrator, created the ornament drawings in the glossary.

Preservation Alliance of Minnesota, the fiscal agent for this book, supported our fundraising efforts, and Richard Lokensgard created an outstanding video for fundraising through giveMN.org.

I am deeply grateful for the financial assistance with writers' and printing fees provided by these donors: Sheila Mitchell, Rosita Wright, Renata Winsor, Alice Melvin, Rolf Anderson, Susan Harker Brunn, TEA 2 Architects, Amy and John Higgins, The Sweatt Foundation, The HRK Foundation, Gary and Karen Kirt, Bell Mortgage, HGA Foundation, Linda Sachs, Larry and Pat Frattallone, Larry and Mary Haeg, Scott and Susan Johnson, and Harold Prowse.

Last but not least, many thanks to the good people of St. Paul, who are somehow all connected through friends, family, religious affiliations, history, and locale. It's true that St. Paul people love their houses, and it shows in the way they lovingly restore them. Special thanks to all the homeowners who opened up their houses to us so that readers could appreciate their preservation efforts firsthand. Their hospitality and willingness to share their houses serve as an inspiration to us all.

Glossary

Illustrations by Narda Lebo

AARON'S ROD a staff entwined with leaves or a snake

ABACUS the uppermost member of a capital, having the appearance of a flat slab on which the entablature rests

ABUTMENT a structure, typically of masonry, that supports a weight and counteracts the lateral thrust of a vault, an arch, or another force

ACANTHUS a plant whose large, stylized, scalloped leaves on a curving stem are commonly found on Corinthian and composite capitals and whose leaves and flowers are often used on other carved ornaments

ACCOLADE an ornamental treatment composed of two ogee curves rising to a central finial, typically found over a door, a window, or an arched opening

ANTHEMION a leaf ornament resembling a fan and based on the radiating blossoms of the honeysuckle or palmette plant, used singly or as a running ornament, often alternating with the lotus

ARABESQUE an intricate ornament, carved, inlaid, sculpted, or painted and composed of an overall pattern of various combinations of intertwined plant and geometric forms

ARCADE a series of arches supported by columns, piers, or pilasters

ARCH a self-supporting structure that spans an opening, usually rounded and composed of voussoirs (types: Arabic, bell, blunt, corbel, depressed, discharging, drop, elliptical, equilateral, flat, Florentine, foiled, four-centered, gauged, Gothic, horseshoe, Indian, Islamic, jack, lancet, Moorish, ogee, one-centered, parabolic, pointed, Queen Anne, rampant, relieving, round, rowlock, segmental, semicircular, shouldered, soldier, splayed, stepped, stilted, straight, Syrian, three-centered, trefoil, triangular, Tudor, two-centered, and Venetian)

ARCHITRAVE the lowest member of an entablature, being the beam that spans from column to column, resting on the capitals

AWNING WINDOW a window that is hinged at the top and swings outward

BALCONETTE a false balcony, typically small in size, or an ornamental railing at a window

BALL FLOWER an ornament composed of three petals enclosing a ball, typically used in moldings

BALLOON FRAMING wood-frame construction whose vertical structural members extend the full height of the two-story frame at the exterior walls

BALUSTER one of a series of short posts, typically circular in section and often quite ornamental, used to support a hand rail or coping and forming a balustrade; also called a banister or a spindle

BALUSTRADE a series of balusters and the handrail or coping they support, or a structure similarly composed, the composition acting as a railing, fence, parapet, or enclosure, often decorative in character

BARGEBOARD a board or other covering, often decorative, hung from the edge of a gable roof to hide the rafters or beams; also called a vergeboard or a gableboard

BARREL ROOF a roof with a semicircular cross section

BARREL VAULT a vault with a semicircular cross-section, held on parallel supports, and extending a considerable length; also called a semicircular vault or a tunnel vault

BASKETWEAVE a masonry bond or ornamental treatment resembling the woven pattern of a basket

BAY one of a series of principal uniform architectural divisions, usually vertically oriented, formed by principal structural members such as columns, often including fenestration; a division of vaulting marked by two transverse ribs

BAY WINDOW a window with a polygonal shape that projects from the exterior surface of a wall, typically rising from the ground

BEAD / BEAD MOLDING a semicircular, convex molding; a molding composed of a series of round or elongated elements

BEAM a main horizontal structural framing member that supports a transverse load

BEAUX-ARTS characterized by the use of historic forms, rich decorative detail, and a tendency toward monumental conception combining Greek, Roman, and Renaissance ideas; buildings are massive, made of stone with columns, balustrades, cornices, pilasters, arches, excess interior ornamentation, and a grand stairway

BELFRY the room at the top of a bell tower that contains the bells

BELL TOWER a tower that houses bells, either separate from or attached to another building

BELVEDERE a building or part of a building, usually at roof level, that commands a view

BLIND blank, having no opening (said of architectural members that are typically open, like windows, arches, etc., but do not function and are applied to a wall to complete a design)

BOARD AND BATTEN wall covering consisting of joined, flush vertical boards, with the joints covered by narrow, vertical wood strips called battens

BOSS a small projecting, richly carved ornament, often incorporating foliage, located at the intersection of members (such as ribs) or at the termination of members (such as moldings or dripstones)

BOUQUET the floral ornament at the top of a finial

BOW WINDOW a bay window with a curved plan

BRACKET a general term for a member, often treated with scrolls or ornament, projecting from a wall and intended to support a weight, as a cornice, etc.; sometimes reserved for wooden support members such as are often found in porches of Victorian-era residences; when used in a series, the series is called bracketing

BROKEN PEDIMENT a triangular pediment whose peak is missing, the empty space often filled with an ornamental feature

BUCRANE, BUCRANIUM an ornament in the form of the head or skull of an ox, often accompanied by a garland and typically used on friezes, especially of the Doric order

BULL'S EYE a small, circular or oval window or other opening

BUTTRESS a structure, typically of masonry, projecting from a wall and counteracting the thrust of an arch, vault, roof, or other structure

C

CAMPANILE a bell tower separate from the main church building, usually Italian in nature

CANEPHORA a figure resembling a young woman supporting a basket on her head

CAPITAL the topmost member of a column, pilaster, etc., which takes a variety of forms and typically carries an architrave, arcade, etc.

CARTOUCHE a panel or shield, often inscribed at the center and provided with an ornamented frame shaped like a scroll or curled paper

CARYATID the figure of a woman used as a support in place of a column

CASEMENT a hinged window that swings open to the side

CAULICOLE in a Corinthian capital, the stalk that rises from the acanthus leaves and supports the volutes

CHAIR RAIL a horizontal interior molding placed at the height of a chair back to protect the wall or at the top of a dado

CHERUB a sculpted figure, often a child with wings, used as ornament

CHEVRON MOLDING a molding composed of a series of V-shaped figures; also called zigzag molding

CHICAGO WINDOW a horizontal window composed of a central, fixed, single pane flanked by narrower sash, often double-hung

CHIMNEY CAP / CHIMNEY HOOD a covering that shelters the opening of a chimney

CHIMNEY POT an ornamental, often cylindrically shaped extension of a flue above the chimney top

CHISEL SHINGLES shingles that are triangular in shape with the point of one shingle centered over the triangle below

CINQUEFOIL an element composed of five foils and five cusps

CLAPBOARD an exterior horizontal wood siding applied so that the thicker edge of each board overlaps the board below; a type of weatherboard

CLASSICAL describing architecture based on the styles of Hellenic Greece and/or Imperial Rome, or the Greek and Roman architecture itself

CLOCK TOWER a tower whose main purpose is the housing of a clock in a prominent position

COFFER one of a series of deeply recessed, polygonal ceiling panels, often highly ornamented; also called a lacunar

COLONNADE a series of columns carrying an entablature and possibly a roof

COMPOSITE one of the five Classical orders of architecture, being an elaboration of the Corinthian order

CONSOLE a version of a bracket, often decorative, in the form of a vertical scroll of greater height than depth, projecting from a wall to support a cornice or other member

COPING the uppermost course of a wall or parapet, typically sloping to shed water and protect the wall below

CORBEL a projecting stone or brick, often used in a series (called corbelling), with each member stepped progressively forward, used to support another member

CORINTHIAN one of the five Classical orders of architecture, characterized by a capital with volutes rising from acanthus leaves

CORNERSTONE a stone prominently placed near the base of a corner of a building to commemorate the date of construction, the architect, and other important information

CORNICE the uppermost division of an entablature; a horizontal ornamental molding at the top of a building or other prominent architectural element, such as a window or door

CORNUCOPIA ornament representing a horn filled with fruit

CRENEL the open space between two merlons in a battlement; also called an embrasure

CRENELLATED MOLDING a molding composed of notches representing merlons and crenels

CRICKET a small projecting structure placed on a sloping roof to divert water away from joints

CROCKET an ornament carved to resemble leaves, flowers, or bunches of foliage, used to decorate the angles of spires, pinnacles, or sloping or vertical edges

CROWN a decorative terminal element the top of an arch

CROWN MOLDING any molding forming the topmost finishing member of a structure or architectural feature

CRUCIFORM shaped like a cross

CUPOLA a rooftop structure, typically composed of a dome on a circular or polygonal base, simple or elaborate in design, small or large in size, originally intended to provide ventilation but sometimes strictly decorative

CURTAIL STEP a step with rounded ends, typically found at the bottom of a flight of stairs

CURTAIN WALL a non-load-bearing exterior wall, applied in front of a framed structure and not supported by its beams or girders; called a window wall if composed primarily of glass

CUSP in tracery, a point made by the joining of two foils

D

DADO the part of a pedestal between the base and the surbase (also called a die) a covering for the lower part of an interior wall, between the baseboard and the chair rail

DART the pointed member between the oval elements in egg and dart ornament; also called an arrowhead

DENTIL one of a series of small, square, tooth-like blocks forming a molding that is used typically in cornices

DOGTOOTH one of a series of diagonally placed ornamental elements taking the form of four leaves radiating from a raised center; also called tooth ornament; a molding consisting of a series of dogtooth ornaments

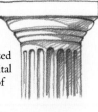

DORIC one of the five Classical orders of architecture, characterized by a simple cushion capital and a frieze composed of triglyphs and metopes

DORMER a window built into a sloping roof with a roof of its own, in a variety of shapes including bowed, flared, flat, gabled, half-round, hipped, jerkinhead, lucerne, pedimented, round headed, segmental, shaped gable, or shed

DOUBLE-HUNG WINDOW / DOUBLE-HUNG SASH WINDOW a window composed of two sashes that slide vertically past each other to close different parts of the window opening

DOUBLE POCKET DOORS two doors that slide in opposite directions into openings in a wall

DOUBLE RETURN STAIR a stair that divides in two after an intermediate landing

DOVETAIL any member with two sides that flare into a wedge shape, especially one intended to fit a joint

DRIP / DRIP MOLDING / DRIPSTONE a projecting molding with a groove on its underside to divert water away from the wall below or a molding resembling such an element; also called a hood molding

DUTCH DOOR a door divided into two independently operating parts, one above the other; also called a stable door

EAVES the overhanging part of a sloping roof

EGG AND DART a molding consisting of egg-shaped elements alternating with arrow- or dart-like elements; also called egg and anchor, egg and arrow, egg and tongue

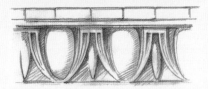

EGG AND LEAF a molding consisting of egg-shaped elements alternating with leaflike elements

EIGHT-OVER-EIGHT a window light arrangement composed of a sash divided into eight panes above another sash divided into eight panes

ELEVATION a wall of a building

ELLIPTICAL STAIR a stair that winds around an elliptical newel or well or a stair whose plan takes the shape of an ellipse

END WALL CHIMNEY a chimney constructed on the end wall of a building but visible only above the ridge of the roof

ENTABLATURE the horizontal member composed of an architrave, a frieze, and a cornice and typically carried by columns or pilasters but also used with other architectural features such as doors and windows

ESCROLL a scroll or ribbon with scrolled ends, typically inscribed and used as ornament on an architectural feature

EXPOSED RAFTERS rafters that extend beyond the wall of a building and are not enclosed by a soffit or other trim

EYE the center of a volute; an oculus at the peak of a dome

EYEBROW a low dormer with no vertical sides and a roof that takes the form of a wave, the roof covering running continuous with that of the main building

FAÇADE the front wall of a building or any architecturally distinguished wall of a building or a wall that stands separate from the building behind, suggesting a building of differerent size or character

FACING a material applied to a wall to finish it and provide a more attractive surface than that underneath, as in siding or veneer

FAN VAULT a vault with ribs that radiate like the ribs of a fan

FANLIGHT a window, usually semicircular in shape, located above a door or window, often with mullions radiating like a fan; also called a lunette

FASCIA / FACIA the broad, flat board that covers the ends of rafters; in Classical architecture, the plain horizontal band of an architrave

FESTOON an ornament consisting of a garland of fruits and flowers, heavy in the middle and suspended at both ends; also called a swag or an encarpus

FIELDSTONE building stone used in its rough, irregular shape, as found in the field

FINIAL an ornament typically consisting of a bunch of foliage that terminates a spire, pinnacle, or other upward-oriented member

FISH SCALE shingles whose lower edges form half-circles (also called half-circle shingles) and overlap to resemble the scales of fish

FLAT ROOF a roof with no perceptible slope

FLEUR-DE-LIS an ornament composed of three pointed members, the center one upright and the sides curved outward, all separated by a horizontal bar from three similar members, or a single vertical one below

FLUTE one of a series of vertical parallel grooves, typically used in the shafts of columns but also used in moldings

FLYING BUTTRESS a buttress often used in architecture of the Gothic period, composed of a solid vertical member and a sloping member that is carried on an arch and connects the vertical member with the wall, intended to absorb the lateral thrust of the roof

FOLIAGE ornament that represents leaves

FOLIATE / FOLIATED ornamented with leaves or leaflike elements

FRENCH DOORS a pair of glass doors that opens in the middle

FRIEZE the member of an entablature located between the architrave and cornice, may be plain or ornamented with sculpted figures or foliage, or triglyphs and metopes, depending on the order used; a long, narrow, horizontal band, typically treated with continuous ornament and located near the top of a wall

G

GABLE / GABLE ROOF / GABLED ROOF a roof having two slopes that meet at a ridge and form a triangle; the triangular part of a wall under a pitched roof, from cornice to peak, often ornamented (types: asymmetrical, closed, crowstep, Dutch, open, and shaped)

GADROONING ornament consisting of a series of non-parallel convex curves; also called nulling or reeding

GAMBREL ROOF a roof with two pitches on each side, the lower pitch being steeper

GARGOYLE a carved ornament representing a grotesquely formed animal, traditionally serving as a waterspout and commonly used as ornament near the roof

GARLAND ornament composed of leaves, fruits, and flowers woven together in a band or wreath

GLAZED furnished with glass

GOOSENECK the curved or angled part of a handrail that meets a newel or turns a corner

GRIFFIN an imaginary creature typically composed of the paws of a lion and the wings and beak of an eagle

GUILLOCHE an ornament composed of two or more curved bands that continuously intertwine, creating round openings that are often filled with ornament

H

HALF TIMBERING a type of construction composed of exposed timber framing, the spaces filled with masonry or plaster

HELIX the volute of a Corinthian or Ionic capital

HERRINGBONE a zigzag pattern, often used ornamentally

HIP KNOB a finial located on a ridge or at the point of a gable where bargeboards meet, often ending in a pendant

HIP ROOF / HIPPED ROOF a roof in which all four sides slope upward, forming four hips

HOPPER WINDOW a window sash that opens inward and is hinged at the bottom or sides

I

IMBRICATION overlapping rows of shingles or other elements of various shapes producing a pattern, often colorful, resembling overlapping scales; also called scale ornament

INGLENOOK a recessed space next to a fireplace, usually housing a bench or opposing benches

INSET DORMER a dormer, the structure of which is partially contained within and below the roof line

IONIC one of the five Classical orders of architecture, characterized by a capital composed of two volutes

J

JALOUSIE WINDOW a window composed of a series of thin, narrow strips of glass that adjust for ventilation

JAMB the vertical member at the sides of a door or window frame

JETTIED a timber-framed building whose upper story overhangs the lower story

JERKINHEAD a roof, the lower half of which is gabled, the upper half of which is angled back to the ridge to form a small hip; also called a clipped gable or hipped gable

K

KEYSTONE the central voussoir of an arch; the middle of an archivolt, often elaborately embellished

L

LANCET / LANCET WINDOW a narrow window in the form of a sharply pointed arch

LANTERN a rooftop structure typically polygonal in plan and of tall, slender proportions, with openings on its sides to light the interior, possibly composing the upper portion of a cupola, or a similar structure used for decorative purposes

LATTICEWORK a pattern composed of members crossing each other orthogonally, diagonally, or curvilinearly

LEADED GLASS / LEADED LIGHT / LEADED WINDOW a window composed of rectangular or diamond-shaped panes of clear or stained glass set in lead cames

LEAF AND DART a molding composed of a series of alternating leaflike figures and darts; also called leaf and tongue

LIGHT a single piece of glass in a door or window; also called a pane

LINCRUSTA embossed wallpaper intended to be painted and varnished, popular from the late 19th century

LINEN PANEL a panel with a treatment representing a piece of cloth laid in vertical folds, from the Tudor period

LINTEL a horizontal member located above an opening, such as a door or window opening, to carry the weight of the wall above

LOTUS a water lily represented in ornament, often stylized as an upright, open flower

LOUVER a system of overlapping horizontal slats placed in an opening to regulate ventilation

LOZENGE a decorative element, usually one of a series, in the shape of a diamond or a square set diagonally

LUCARNE / LUCERNE a small dormer window, especially one whose face takes the shape of a segment of a circle and whose roof is distinct from the roof of the main building

LUNETTE a semicircular or crescent-shaped window

M

MANSARD / MANSARD ROOF a roof having two slopes on all four sides, the lower slope steeper and longer than the upper slope, popularized by French architect Francois Mansart

MASCARON / MASK an ornament representing a grotesque human or a partly human face or head, often used on keystones, etc.

MEDALLION an ornamental tablet, panel, or plaque, typically oval in shape and providing the background for a carved figure

MISSION TILE a semi-cylindrical roofing tile made of clay and laid with convex sides alternately up and down

MODILLION a version of a bracket, of greater depth than height and used in a series, often taking the form of a scroll decorated on the underside with an acanthus leaf, especially when part of a Corinthian cornice

MOLDING a decorative member of long proportion, shaped into one of a variety of contours to introduce variations of light, shade, and shadow into a design (types: anthemion, ballflower, base, bay leaf garland, bead, bead and quirk, bead and reel, billet, bird's beak, bolection, bowtell, brace, cavetto, chain, chamfer, chevron, corner bead, crenellated, crown, cyma recta, cyma reversa, dogtooth, drip, edge roll, egg and dart, fillet, flush bead, fluting, fret, heart and dart, hollow chamfer, hollow square, indented, interrupted arch, label, lattice, leaf and dart, lozenge, medallion, nailhead, nebule, necking, open heart, ovolo, pearl, pellet, picture, prismatic billet, quarter hollow, quarter round, quirk, reeding, reed and tie, reticulated, roll and fillet, roll billet, rope, rose, sawtooth, scotia, scroll, segmental billet, sprung, square billet, star, struck, sunk fillet, tablet flower, three-quarter round, torus, Vitruvian scroll, and wave)

MOIRÉ fabric or wallpaper, usually silk that has a wavelike pattern or watered look

MULLION the vertical member that divides multiple windows or doors in a single opening, the lights of a window, or the panels of a door

MUNTIN a small, slender mullion; a secondary framing member that divides the panes of a window or the panels of a door

N

NEWEL / NEWEL POST the post at the top, bottom, and turning points of a stair, typically larger and more elaborate than the balusters; the central upright post around which a circular staircase winds

NICHE a recess in a wall, often with a curved plan, to hold a statue, vase, etc.

NOGGING a type of construction in which a timber frame is infilled with brickwork

O

OBELISK a tall, slender structure with a square plan and sloping sides ending in a pyramid; a similar form used ornamentally; a dome composed of eight curved sections

OCULUS the opening at the peak of a dome

OGEE an S-curved line composed of a convex and a concave part, typically used on moldings and ornament

ONION DOME a pointed, bulbous roof

OPEN EAVES eaves in which the triangular space between the rafters and the exterior wall is not enclosed but in which an inclined soffit is attached to the rafters, creating a continuous surface

OPEN STRING a string whose top edge matches the profile of the stairs

ORIEL a bay window at an upper story, supported by corbels, brackets, or an engaged column or pier

ORMOLU golden or gilded brass or bronze used for decorative purposes

ORNAMENT any feature added to a structure or member for decorative effect

OVAL WINDOW a window that takes the shape of an oval

OVERDOOR a decorated panel directly above a door

OX EYE WINDOW a window that takes the shape of a long ellipse

P

PALLADIAN WINDOW a large window arrangement divided into three parts by columns, pilasters, etc., with flat lintels at the sides flanking a taller arched central lintel; also called a Diocletian window, Serlian window, or Venetian window

PANELED DOOR / PANELED SHUTTER a door/shutter with stiles, rails, and possibly muntins forming frames around panels

PANTILE a roofing tile with an S-shaped section

PARAPET the vertical extension of an exterior wall above the line of the roof, often decorated

PATERA a small disk decorated with leaves or petals, used in panels, friezes, etc.

PEDESTAL a substructure for a column, statue, etc., often composed of a base, dado, and cornice

PEDIMENT the gable end of a roof, often triangular or segmentally shaped, located over a portico and above the cornice in Classical architecture; a similar feature above doors and windows, etc. (types: broken pediment, open bed pediment, Queen Anne arch pediment, segmental pediment, and swan's neck pediment)

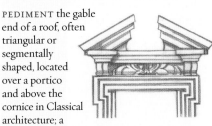

PENDANT a suspended hanging ornament, often richly decorated; also called a drop ornament

PICTURE MOLDING a horizontal, interior molding from which pictures are hung, or a molding placed at such a height

PIER a vertical structural member more massive than a column, often square or rectangular in plan, that supports a load; a supporting member that comprises a substantial part of a wall

PILASTER a pier engaged with its base, shaft, and capital but providing no support, typically rectangular in plan

PILLAR a columnlike member, isolated or providing support that does not conform to the Classical rules of architecture

PINNACLE a vertical structure, tapering as it rises, being the ornamental terminating feature of a buttress, parapet, gable, etc.

PITCH the degree of the slope of a roof or other surface

PLINTH / PLINTH BLOCK the square block below the base of a column, pilaster, wall, or door framing, connecting it with the ground or sill, typically treated with moldings or other ornament

POCKET DOORS doors that open by sliding into openings in the wall so that they are hidden when completely open

POPPYHEAD, POPPY a finial in the shape of a fleur-de-lis or carved with foliage, flowers, or other ornament

PORTE COCHERE from the French term for carriage porch, a structure extending from the roof over a driveway, used for shelter when exiting or entering the building to or from a vehicle

PORTICO a colonnade supporting a roof at the entrance to a building, distinguished by number and placement of columns (types: amphiprostyle, anta, astylar, decastyle, dipteral, distyle, distyle in antis, dodecastyle, enneastyle, heptastyle, hexastyle, monopteral, octastyle, pentastyle, peripteral, prostyle, pseudodipteral, pseudoperipteral, tetrastyle, and tripteral)

PURLIN a horizontal wooden roof framing member that connects the principal rafters of a roof

PUTTO a figure of a child without wings

Q

QUARRY GLASS a small diamond-shaped pane of glass, typically used in leaded windows

QUARTER ROUND WINDOW a window that takes that shape of one quarter of a circle

QUATREFOIL an element composed of four foils with four cusps

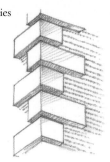

QUEEN ANNE an architectural style popular from 1880 to 1910, characterized by steep roofs, complicated asymmetrical shapes, front-facing gables, one-story porches that extend across one or two sides of the house, round or square towers, exterior surfaces textured with decorative shingles, patterned masonry, ornamental spindles and brackets, and bay windows

QUIRK a V-shaped groove between moldings

QUOIN one of a series of alternately large and small masonry units that typically form the corner of a building and are often distinguished from the adjacent masonry by varying surface treatment; French for corner

R

RAFTER one of a series of inclined wooden framing members that form the structure of a roof

RAIL a horizontal member in the frame of a door or window (types: bottom rail, meeting rail, and top rail); a handrail

RAISED PANEL a panel with a plain central area raised above the surrounding edge or frame; also called a fielded panel

REED one of a series of small, parallel, convex moldings representing a bunch of reeds, being the opposite of fluting

RETICULATED ornamented with a network of regularly intersecting lines

RETURN the continuation of a member that turns away at an angle from the main part of the member onto an adjacent surface

REVEAL the side of a door or window opening between the door or window frame and the outer surface of the wall; when cut diagonally it is called a splay

RIB a curved member, typically molded, forming the structure on which a vault is built

RIBBED VAULT a vault supported by ribs

RINCEAU ORNAMENT composed of vines and foliage intertwined, often in scroll-like forms and combined with other ornament

RISE the vertical distance from the springing line of an arch to the crown of the arch; the vertical distance between two consecutive treads in a stair, being the height of the riser

RISER the vertical part of a step

ROCK-FACED stone with a natural stone face or a face dressed to resemble that of natural stone; also called rough-faced

ROMAN IONIC an Ionic capital with volutes projecting diagonally

ROOF the structure that covers a building (types: asymmetrical gable, barrel, bell, broach, conical, cross gable, dome, Dutch gable, Dutch gambrel, flared, flat, gable, gambrel, helm, hip, hip and valley, jerkinhead, lean-to, mansard, monitor, pavilion, pitched, polygonal hip, pyramidal, rainbow, salt box, sawtooth, shed, single-pitch, and whaleback)

ROSETTE a carved, rounded ornament resembling a flower

ROTUNDA a structure with a circular plan and a domical roof

ROW HOUSE one of a row of houses that share sidewalls

RUSTICATION massive blocks of cut masonry separated by deeply recessed, strongly emphasized joints; the faces of the block may be rock-faced (appearing as if straight from the quarry), diamond-pointed, paneled, or vermiculated; flat, hand- or machine-tooled; the border of each block may be chamfered or beveled on two or four sides

S

SASH the unit that holds the window glass, especially when sliding in vertical grooves

SASH WINDOW a (typically double-hung) window that opens by sliding vertically or is hung by chains or sash cords over pulleys in the frame

SCALLOP ornament representing a ribbed shell

SCROLL ORNAMENT in the form of a wound spiral, often applied singly to brackets or joined continuously in a molding, typically called a Vitruvian scroll

SCROLLWORK any ornamental work composed, at least in part, of scrolls

SHAKE a thick, tapered wood shingle, typically split by hand

SHED DORMER a dormer with a shed roof and eaves parallel to that of the main roof

SHED ROOF a roof with a single slope; also called a pent roof

SHINGLE a type of roof covering consisting of small units produced in standard sizes and in a variety of materials and shapes, laid in overlapping courses to prevent water infiltration (types: chisel, cove, diamond, fish scale, half-circle, hexagonal, horizontal, octagonal, plain, round, sawtooth, segmental, square, square wave, and staggered; *see also*: imbrication)

SHUTTER a small, hinged door that covers a window or other opening

SIDELIGHT a slender, vertical window, typically one of a pair flanking a door

SILL the bottom, horizontal framing member of a door or window opening; when covering the joint between two types of flooring material, it is called a saddle or threshold; the horizontal framing member at the bottom of a timber-framed wall

SINGLE PANE WINDOW a window composed of one pane of glass, either fixed or operable

SIX-OVER-ONE a window light arrangement composed of a sash divided into six panes above a sash composed of a single pane

SIX-OVER-SIX a window light arrangement composed of a sash divided into six panes above another sash divided into six panes

SKYLIGHT a glazed opening in a roof, in one of a variety of shapes, to admit light and possibly ventilation to the space below (types: dome, flat, pyramid, single pitch, ridge, square dome, vault, and venting)

SLIDING DOOR / SLIDING WINDOW / SLIDING SASH a door or window that slides horizontally in a track

SLIT WINDOW a window whose proportions are tall and narrow

SNOW BIRD / SNOW GUARD one of a number of elements, often decorative, attached to a roof in a regular pattern to prevent snow from sliding off the slope

SPAN the width of an arch or the distance between two consecutive supporting elements

SPANDREL the space between windows of adjacent stories; the triangular area bounded by the outer curve of an arch, a horizontal line drawn from the crown of the arch, and a vertical line drawn from the springing point; in a stair string, the triangular area between the tread and riser

SPANISH TILE a semi-cylindrical roofing tile made of clay and laid with the convex side up

SPHINX a figure with the body of a lion and a human head

SPIDER WEB FANLIGHT a fanlight with a pattern of mullions that resembles a spider web

SPINDLE a baluster made of wood, often turned

SPIRAL COLUMN a column treated with fluting that continuously winds around the shaft

SPIRAL STAIR a flight of stairs with a circular plan and treads wound around a central newel; also called a circular stair or newel stair

SPIRE a tall, slender, pointed structure built on a roof or tower

SPUR an ornamental element, often in the form of a leaf or grotesque figure, joining the base of a round column to its polygonal plinth

SQUINCH a system of arches or corbelling built across the corners of a square space to support a polygonal or domed roof

STAINED GLASS WINDOW a window composed partially or completely of panes of colored glass

STAIR a structure composed of a tread and a riser and used in a series to bridge the distance from one level to another (types: box, closed string, dogleg, double, double return, elliptical, geometrical, open newel, open riser, open string, ramp, spiral, straight run, and stoop)

STEEPLE the tower and spire of a church or a similar ornamental rooftop structure that diminishes in size as it rises

STEP a riser and a tread

STICKWORK a type of construction in which a timber framework is filled or partially filled with wooden boards, often placed at angles

STOOP a short series of steps leading to the entrance of a house or other building

STRAIGHT RUN STAIR a stair that has no turns and travels in only one direction

STRIATED describing a surface or element treated with courses or layers of varying color, texture, size, or elevation

STRINGCOURSE a continuous horizontal band, typically molded and projecting from the face of a building; also called a belt course

STUCCO an exterior wall finish composed of cement, lime, sand, and water

SUNBURST ornament resembling the sun and its rays, often used in gables

SURROUND a decorative window or door frame, including the lintel, sill, hood, and any other associated features

SWAN'S NECK PEDIMENT a broken pediment whose sides are S-shaped; also called a scrolled pediment

SWING DOOR a door that swings a full 180 degrees; also called a double-acting door

T

THRESHOLD the member covering the joint between two types of flooring material; also called a saddle or a sill

TONGUE AND GROOVE a joint formed by inserting a continuously projecting part (a tongue) of one member into the groove of another member

TRACERY the ornamental stone or wood framework in a Gothic window or a window based on Gothic design

TRANSOM / TRANSOM LIGHT / TRANSOM WINDOW the hinged window located above a door or a larger window and separated from the door or window by a transom bar

TREAD the horizontal part of a stair on which the foot steps

TREFOIL a member composed of three foils and three cusps

TROMPE L'OEIL to fool the eye; a painted decorative effect of a vista or scene that gives the illusion of reality

TRUSS an arrangement, often triangular, of structural members forming a rigid framework for building construction

TUDOR ARCH a pointed, four-centered arch

TURRET a small tower, typically located at the corner of a building, often supported by corbels

TUSCAN one of the five classical orders of architecture, resembling a simplified version of the Doric

TWISTED COLUMN a column whose shaft is spiral in form; also called a Solomonic column

TYMPANUM the area bounded by a pediment, often decorated

U

URN a vase with a rounded body on a base, traditionally used to contain the ashes of the dead

V

VALLEY the internal angle formed by the intersection of two slopes of a roof or by the slope of a roof and a rooftop element

VANE a metal ornament on a pinnacle, spire, etc., that rotates to indicate the direction of the wind

VAULT a masonry structure based on the arch principle, providing a roof over a given area (types: barrel, coved, cross, domical, double, elliptical, expanding, fan, groin, lierne, pointed, quadripartite, rampant, ribbed, segmental, semicircular, sexpartite, stilted, and tunnel)

VENEER a facing of material, especially masonry, more ornamental in appearance than the material underneath

VENT a device designed to allow for the circulation of air

VENTING SKYLIGHT an operable skylight, used to increase ventilation in the space below

VERANDA a roof-covered but open porch, gallery, or balcony supported by posts

VERNACULAR term describing rural architecture with little or no stylistic pretension

VITRUVIAN SCROLL a frieze ornament made up of a series of wavelike scrolls; also referred to as a running dog

VOLUTE a spiral scroll, especially the one forming the characteristic element of the Ionic capital; also called a helix

VOUSSOIR a masonry unit, typically wedge-shaped, used to construct an arch

W

WAINSCOT facing applied to the lower part of an interior wall, often below a chair rail

WAVE MOLDING a molding composed of a series of figures representing breaking waves

WICKET a small door within a larger one

WIDOW'S WALK a narrow platform on a roof, typically surrounded by a railing or balustrade; also called a captain's walk

WINDING STAIR a stair composed chiefly of winders, as in a spiral stair

WINDOW a glazed opening in an exterior wall that admits light and air (types: accordion, awning, bay, blind, bow, box head, bull's eye, casement, Chicago, classroom, cruciform, Diocletian, dormer, double-hung, double lancet, drop, fanlight, fixed, hopper, horizontal pivot, hung, jalousie, lancet, lunette, multi-pane, octagonal, oval, ox eye, Palladian, quarter round, Queen Anne, round headed, sash, Serlian, shouldered, show, skylight, sliding, splayed, stained glass, transom, utility, Venetian, vertical pivot, and wheel)

WRAPAROUND PORCH a porch constructed so as to continue from one side of a building to another

WREATH an ornament taking the form of a circular garland of flowers, fruits, leaves, etc.

Z

ZIGZAG a line with a continuous series of sharply angled turns, used for ornamental effect, as in herringbone-bond and chevron moldings

ZOOPHORIC a column supporting a sculpture of an animal

From *Architecture and Ornament: An Illustrated Dictionary* ©2009 [1997] Margaret Maliszweski-Pickart by permission of McFarland & Company, Inc., Box 611, Jefferson NC 28640. www.mcfarlandpub.com

Sources

General

Calloway, Stephen, and Elizabeth Cromley, eds. *The Elements of Style: A Practical Encyclopedia of Interior Architectural Details from 1485 to the Present.* New York: Simon and Schuster, 1991 (rev. ed., 1997).

Gebhard, David, and Tom Martinson. *Architecture of Minnesota.* Minneapolis: University of Minnesota Press, 1977.

Hess, Jeffrey, and Larson, Paul Clifford. *St. Paul's Architecture: A History.* Minneapolis: University of Minnesota Press, 2006.

Lathrop, Alan K. *Minnesota Architects: A Biographical Dictionary.* Minneapolis: University of Minnesota Press, 2010.

McAlester, Virginia, and Lee McAlester. *A Field Guide to American Houses.* New York: Knopf, 2005.

Marquis, Albert Nelson. *The Book of Minnesotans: A Biographical Dictionary of the Leading Living Men in the State of Minnesota.* Chicago: A. N. Marquis, 1907.

Millett, Larry. *AIA Guide to St. Paul's Summit Avenue and Hill District.* St. Paul: Minnesota Historical Society Press, 2009.

Sandeen, Ernest R. *St. Paul's Historic Summit Avenue.* Minneapolis: University of Minnesota Press, 2004 (originally published in 1978).

Introduction

"A Big Record for St. Paul." *St. Paul Pioneer Press,* Oct. 14, 1883.

Boardman, Kathryn. "Tough Old Summit Fights to Survive." *St. Paul Dispatch,* May 11, 1960.

Bond, John Wesley. *Minnesota and Its Resources.* New York: Redfield, 1853.

Eichern, Katie. "The Crown Jewel of St. Paul: A History of Conservation along Summit Avenue." Honors Paper, Bethel College, Nov. 26, 2012.

Map of the City of St. Paul, Capital of Minnesota. St. Paul, MN: Goodrich and Somers, 1857.

"St. Paul." *The Northwest* 2 (June 1884).

"Summit Avenue Called the Pinnacle of U.S. Streets." *Minneapolis StarTribune,* Oct. 8, 2008.

"Summit Boulevard." *St. Anthony Graphic.* Oct 4, 1889.

Wellge, H. *St. Paul, Minnesota 1883: State Capital and County Seat of Ramsey Co.* (map). Madison, WI: J. J. Stoner, ca. 1883.

Stuart–Driscoll House

"At the Mayor's House." *St. Paul Globe,* Oct. 12, 1887, p. 1.

Cass Gilbert Society. "Driscoll House." Accessed July 8, 2013. http://www.cassgilbertsociety.org/works/stpaul-driscoll-312summit.

Kenney, Dave. Interviews with and information from Steve Balej and Jim Sazevich, April 10, 2013.

Martin, Lawrence A., comp. "Thursday Night Hikes: Summit Avenue East Hike, Architecture Notes 2." Accessed July 8, 2013. http://www.angelfire.com/mn/thursdaynighthikes/summiteast2.html.

Burbank–Livingston–Griggs House

Rich, Frieda, and Lael Berman. *Landmarks Old and New: Minneapolis and St. Paul and Surrounding Areas.* Minneapolis: Nodin, 1988.

Illustrated Historical Atlas of the State of Minnesota. Chicago: A. T. Andreas, 1874.

Jacobsen, Christina H. "The Burbank–Livingston–Griggs House." *Minnesota History* 42, no. 1 (Spring 1970).

Koeper, H. F. *Historic St. Paul Buildings.* St. Paul, MN: St. Paul City Planning Board, 1964.

Larson, Paul Clifford. *Minnesota Architect: The Life and Work of Clarence Johnston.* Afton, MN: Afton Historical Society Press, 1996.

National Register of Historic Places. National Park Service. 2007-01-23.

"St. Paul Architecture," *St. Paul Pioneer Press,* June 10, 1883.

St. Paul Building Permits 32575 (1895), 33345 (1896), 16714 (1925). Ramsey County Historical Society Archives.

St. Paul City Directory. St. Paul, MN: R. L. Polk, 1861–1884.

"St. Paul Illustrated," *St. Paul Daily Globe,* Dec. 31, 1883.

Silverman, Eleni. "James C. Burbank House." Historic American Buildings Survey. Library of Congress, 1984.

U.S. Census, 1870, 1880, 1900.

Williams, John Fletcher. *A History of the City of Saint Paul, and of the County of Ramsey, Minnesota.* St. Paul: Minnesota Historical Society, 1876.

A. G. Manson House

Hammel, Bette. Interviews with and information from interior designer Shari Wilsey and owner Jessica Stoltenberg (June 23, 2013), and former owners Sen. David Durenburger and Susan Foote (June 25, 2013).

Historic Sites Survey of 649 Summit, 1976. Minnesota State Historic Preservation Office.

Historic Sites Survey of 649 Summit, June 7, 1982. St. Paul Heritage Preservation Commission and Ramsey County Historical Society.

Summerson, John. *The Classical Language of Architecture.* London/New York: Thames and Hudson, 1980.

Cyrus B. Thurston House

"Avenue of Barons." *Twin Cities.* (Undated news clipping regarding second owner, Schiffman, ca. 1967)

Hammel, Bette. Interview with and information from Sheila Moar, May 27, 2013.

Historic Sites Survey, Jan. 1976. Minnesota Historical Society.

Historic Sites Survey of 495 Summit Avenue, May 27, 1982. St. Paul: Ramsey County Historical Society and St. Paul Heritage Preservation Commission.

Johnston, Clarence (file). Northwest Architectural Archives, information regarding D. (Denslow) W. Millard plans for Thurston house.

Larson, Paul Clifford. *Minnesota Architect: The Life and Work of Clarence Johnston.* Afton, MN: Afton Historical Society Press, 1996.

Ostman, Eleanor. "House Has Secret Past." *St. Paul Sunday Pioneer Press,* April 4, 1965.

Twin Cities undated news clipping, ca. 1964.

William W. Howard House

Claire T. Carney Library. "Stick Style Architecture." *University of Massachusetts Dartmouth.* Accessed June 20, 2013. http://prior.lib.umassd.edu/digicoll/stickarch/stick_architecture.html.

Encyclopedia Britannica. "Charles Locke Eastlake." *Encyclopedia Britannica Online.* Accessed July 12, 2013. http://www.britannica.com/EBchecked/topi/177428/Charles-Locke-Eastlake.

LaChuisa, Chuck. "Eastlake Style in Buffalo, NY." *Buffalo As Architectural Museum.* Accessed Aug. 14, 2013. http://www.buffaloah.com/a/archsty/east/.

Nelson, Melinda. Interviews with and information from Paul Clifford Larson and owner Roddie Turner, June 2013.

DRISCOLL–WEYERHAEUSER HOUSE

Castle, Henry. "Biographic Memorial of Frederick Driscoll." *Collections of the Minnesota Historical Society* 15 (May 1915), 687–710.

Larson, Paul Clifford. *Minnesota Architect: The Life and Work of Clarence H. Johnston*. Afton, MN: Afton Historical Society Press, 1996.

Lathrop, Alan K. "A French Architect in Minnesota," *Minnesota History* 47 (Summer 1980), 43–56.

Lewis, Arnold. *American Country Houses of the Gilded Age (Sheldon's "Artistic Country-Seats")*. New York: Dover Architecture, 1982.

Minnesota Census, 1895.

Pyle, J. G. *Picturesque St. Paul*. St. Paul, MN: Northwestern Photo, 1888.

St. Paul Building Permits 1522, 1615 (1884), 4378 (1885); (new series) 68078 (1917). Ramsey County Historical Society Archives.

St. Paul City Directory. St. Paul, MN: R. L. Polk, 1880–1917.

U. S. Census, 1880, 1900, 1910, 1920.

Willcox, William H. *Hints to Those Who Propose to Build* (pamphlet). St. Paul, MN: Privately published, 1884.

LAUREL TERRACE—RILEY ROW

Hammel, Bette. Interview with and information from the owners at their townhouse (July 12, 2013) and metalworker/architect John Yust (July 16, 2013).

Historic Structures. "Laurel Terrace, St. Paul, Minnesota." Accessed July 14, 2013. www.historic-structures.com/mn/st_paul/laurel_terrace.php

WILLIAM G. WHITE HOUSE

Nelson, Melinda. Interviews with and information from Paul and Becky Diekmann, Paul Clifford Larson, and Tommy Brandt, July 2013.

Safford, Virginia. "The Home of the North." Edwin Gardner White and Family Papers, Minnesota Historical Society.

White, Edwin G., to Emily Post, n.d. Edwin Gardner White and Family Papers, Minnesota Historical Society.

DIDRIK OMEYER HOUSE

Historic Sites Survey of 808 Goodrich Avenue, 1982. Ramsey County Historical Society and St. Paul Heritage Preservation Commission.

Kenney, Dave. Interview with and information from the owner, June/July 2103.

Millett, Larry. "Recreated Queen Anne Porch," *MARQ*, June/July 2007.

F. SCOTT FITZGERALD HOUSE—SUMMIT TERRACE

"Gables, Gardens and Ghosts." *St. Paul Pioneer Press*, undated 2003 news clipping with photo of homeowners Mike and Nancy Jones.

Hammel, Bette. Interview and tour of home with owners Mike and Nancy Jones, June 3, 2013.

Hampl, Patricia. Introduction to *The St. Paul Stories of F. Scott Fitzgerald*. St. Paul: Minnesota Historical Society Press, 2004.

Ramsey Hill Association. *Gables, Gardens, & Ghosts* (tour brochure including F. Scott Fitzgerald timeline). St. Paul, MN: Author, 2003.

Summerson, John. *The Classical Language of Architecture*. London/New York: Thames and Hudson, 1980

Turnbull, Andrew. *Scott Fitzgerald*. New York: Scribner's, 1962.

WILLIAM & CARRIE LIGHTNER HOUSE

"The Architect." Cass Gilbert Society. Accessed July 11, 2013. http://www.cassgilbertsociety.org/architect/gilbert.html.

City of Saint Paul Heritage Preservation Commission Staff Report. St. Paul, MN: Author, 2006.

Larson, Paul Clifford. "A Home of Versatile Talents: The William and Carrie Lightner Residence, on Summit Avenue." *Ramsey County History*, 42, no. 1 (Spring 2007).

Nelson, Melinda. Interviews with and information from John Fallin, Paul Clifford Larson, and Thomas R. Blanck, July 2013.

"The Showcase Home Tour." *Mpls.St.Paul* insert dated July 13, 2007, p. 11.

THOMAS & MARY CLARE SCOTT HOUSE

Anderson, Diane. "The Talking House." Unpublished monograph in possession of the owner, n.d.

"George Thompson, of St. Paul, Dies." *Editor and Publisher* 49, no. 31 (Jan. 13, 1917): 34.

Kenney, Dave. Interview with and information from Steven Anderson and Diane Anderson, June 24, 2013.

Martin, Lawrence A., comp. "Thursday Night Hikes: Summit Avenue East Hike, Architecture Notes 2." Accessed July 8, 2013. http://www.angelfire.com/mn/thursdaynighthikes/summiteast2.html.

FREDERICK A. FOG HOUSE

Kenney, Dave. Interviews with and info from Larry Frattallone (June 18, 2013) and Tom Harkcom (June 29, 2013).

Millett, Larry. "Mansion Has a New Look for Hill Tour." *St. Paul Pioneer Press*, Sept. 13, 1989.

LOUIS W. HILL HOUSE

Hammel, Bette. Interview with and information from Nancy and Dick Nicholson, May 14, 2013.

Larson, Paul Clifford. *Minnesota Architect: The Life and Work of Clarence Johnston*. Afton, MN: Afton Historical Society Press, 1996.

"Mansion Makeover." *Star Tribune*, Feb. 11, 2004.

Young, Biloine W., with Eileen R. McCormack. *The Dutiful Son: Louis W. Hill*. St. Paul, MN: Ramsey County Historical Society, 2010

CARLOS N. BOYNTON HOUSE

City of Saint Paul Heritage Preservation Commission Certificate of Approval for Work at 955 Summit Avenue, 2013.

Nelson, Melinda. Interviews with and information from Paul Clifford Larson and Roger and Shari Wilsey, June 2013.

SAMUEL & MADELINE DITTENHOFER HOUSE

"Christian Brothers Provincialate." Unpublished paper, Minnesota State Historic Preservation Office, n.d.

Gracious Spaces (DVD.) St. Paul, MN: TPT, 2012.

Historic Sites Survey of 807 Summit Avenue, 1982. Ramsey County Historical Society and St. Paul Heritage Preservation Commission.

Johnston. C. H., ledgers. Commissions 1534 and 1891. Clarence H. Johnston papers. Northwest Architectural Archives.

Larson, Paul Clifford. *Minnesota Architect: The Life and Work of Clarence H. Johnston*. Afton, MN: Afton Historical Society Press, 1996.

Little Sketches of Big Folks. St. Paul, MN: R. L. Polk, 1907.

"Report of the Death of an American Citizen, American Foreign Service" (Paris, August 27, 1952). *Reports of Deaths of American Citizens Abroad, 1835–1974*. Ancestry.com.

"Residence of S. W. Dittenhofer, St. Paul, Minnesota." *Western Architect* 12 (Dec. 1908).

St. Paul Building Permit (new series) 46452 (1907). Ramsey County Historical Society Archives.

A. W. LINDEKE HOUSE

Nelson, Melinda. Interviews with and information from Karen and Lori Kustritz and Paul Clifford Larson, July 2013.

Yale University. *The Yale Banner* 51 (1892). Accessed Aug. 14, 2013. http://books.google.com/books/about/The_Yale_Banner.html?id=XRzOAAAAMAAJ.

CHARLES L. & JENNIE JOHNSTON HOUSE

Castle, Henry Anson. *History of St. Paul and Vicinity: A Chronicle of Progress and a Narrative Account of the Industries, Institutions, and People of the City and Its Tributary Territory*, vol. 3. Chicago: Lewis, 1912.

Little Sketches of Big Folks. St. Paul, MN: R. L. Polk, 1907.

Minnesota Census, 1885.

Progressive Men of Minnesota. Minneapolis: The Minnesota Journal, 1897.

St. Paul Building Permit (new series) 54860 (1910). Ramsey County Historical Society Archives.

St. Paul City Directory. St. Paul: R. L. Polk, 1878–1915.

Sons of the American Revolution Membership Applications, 1889–1970. Louisville, KY: National Society of the Sons of the American Revolution.

U.S. Census, 1880, 1900, 1920, 1940.

GOODKIND BROTHERS DOUBLE HOUSE

Halunen, Clayton. "7 Heather Place, St. Paul, Minnesota." *Placeography.* Accessed July 23, 2013. http://placeography.org/index.php/7_Heather_Place,_St._Paul,_Minnesota.

Linder, James A. *Farms and Fox Hunts: A History of the City of Gem Lake, Minnesota* (2005). Accessed July 16, 2013. http://www.gemlakemn.org/gl_uploads/Gem_Lake_history_V1%5B1%5D.0C.pdf

Nelson, Melinda. Interviews with and information from Clayton Halunen, David Duddingston, and Paul Clifford Larson, June 2013.

BEEBE–LEUTHOLD HOUSE

Hammons, Mark. "Purcell and Elmslie, Architects." In Michael Conforti, ed., *Minnesota 1900: Art and Life on the Upper Mississippi 1890–1915,* 214–98. Newark: University of Delaware Press, 1994.

Kenney, Dave. Interview with Martha Anderson, May 8, 2013.

Legler, Dixie. *At Home on the Prairie: The Houses of Purcell & Elmslie.* San Francisco: Chronicle Books, 2006.

Martin, Lawrence A., comp. "Observations on Architectural Styles: Western Summit Avenue Hike Architecture Notes." Accessed July 8, 2013. http://www.angelfire.com/mn/thursdaynighthikes/summiteast.html.

PAUL & MARY DOTY HOUSE

Haeg, Larry. "The Paul and Mary Doty House." Unpublished booklet, 2011.

Larson, Paul Clifford. *A Walk through Dellwood.* Dellwood, MN: City of Dellwood, 2008.

Lathrop, Alan K. "A French Architect in Minnesota." *Minnesota History* 47, no. 2 (Summer 1980), 42–56.

Little Sketches of Big Folks. St. Paul, MN: R. L. Polk, 1907.

McLean, Robert Craik. "Emmanuel Louis Masqueray." *Western Architect* 25–26 (July 1917).

Masqueray, E. L. "Religious Architecture and the Cathedral of Saint Paul and Pro-Cathedral of the Immaculate Conception." *Western Architect* 12, no. 4 (Oct. 1908).

Matthews' Complete American Armoury and Blue Book. New York: Gorham, 1907.

U.S. Passport Application for Mary Doty, May 18, 1920. Ancestry.com.

LINDSAY–WEYERHAEUSER HOUSE

Historic Sites Survey of 294 Summit Avenue, 1980. Ramsey County Historical Society and St. Paul Heritage Preservation Commission.

Kenney, Dave. Interview with and information from Jenny Nilsson, June 14, 2013.

Twining, Charles E. *F. K. Weyerhaeuser: A Biography.* St. Paul: Minnesota Historical Society Press, 1997.

LOUIS SILVERSTEIN HOUSE

Hammel, Bette. Interviews with and information from owner Karen Olson (June 13, 2013) and architect David Heide (June 20, 2013).

Heide, David. "977 Summit Avenue Project Team" (project overview, 2009–2011). David Heide Design Studio.

The Improvement Bulletin, July 20. 1912, and March 18, 1913.

Linhoof, Peter J., papers. Northwest Architectural Archives, University of Minnesota.

Louis Silverstein (obituary). *St. Paul Pioneer Press,* Jan. 26, 1954.

EGIL & RACHEL BOECKMANN HOUSE

David Adler Archive at the Art Institute of Chicago. Chicago: Art Institute of Chicago, 2000.

Houghton, Frederick Lowell. *Holstein-Friesian Herd-Book,* vol. 43. Brattleboro, VT: Holstein-Friesian Association of America, 1920.

Hutto, Richard Jay. *Their Gilded Cage: The Jekyll Island Club Members.* Macon, GA: Indigo, 2005.

Larson, Paul Clifford. *A Walk through Dellwood.* Dellwood, MN: City of Dellwood, 2008.

Pappas, Al. *Gophers Illustrated: The Incredible Complete History of Minnesota Football.* Minneapolis: University of Minnesota Press, 1909.

Thorne, Martha, ed. *David Adler, Architect: The Elements of Style.* New Haven, CT: Yale University Press, 2002.

U. S. Census, 1910, 1920, 1930.

PHOTO CREDITS

All photos are © 2013 by Karen Melvin except for the following, which are published by permission or are in the public domain:

Photos © 2013 by Philip Prowse: pages 16, 49, 65, 71, 82–83, 108–09, 196–97, 232–33, and 251–53.

Pages 2–3: H. Wellge, *St. Paul, Minnesota 1883: State Capital and County Seat of Ramsey Co.* (map) (Madison, WI: J. J. Stoner, ca. 1883).

Page 3: From *An Illustrated Historical Atlas of the State of Minnesota* (Chicago: A. T. Andreas, 1874).

Page 4: Courtesy of the Minnesota Historical Society.

Page 5: Courtesy of the St. Paul Public Library.

Page 7: From J. G. Pyle, *Picturesque St. Paul* (St. Paul, MN: Northwestern Photo, 1887).

Page 57: From George B. Sheldon, *Artistic Country-Seats* (1886–1887).

Page 185: Postcard (St. Paul, MN: R. Steinman, n.d.).